He Promised He'd Stop

Helping Women
Find Safe Passage from
Abusive Relationships

by

Michael Groetsch

CPI Publishing Brookfield, Wisconsin

NOTE: Many of the stories in this book derive from the author's personal interviews with more than 20,000 batterers and their victims. Others come from written accounts in newpapers and magazines. Names of individuals and citations to source material have been omitted in most cases, and certain facts have been altered to protect the privacy of victims and their families. Anecdotal material taken from published accounts is presented for purposes of illustration only, and the author does not vouch for its accuracy. The conclusions and advice expressed in this book are solely those of the author and do not necessarily reflect the views of the publisher.

© 1997 by CPI Publishing

A division of Crisis Prevention Institute, Inc.

Crisis Prevention Institute, 3315-K N. 124th Street, Brookfield, WI 53005.

Printed in the United States of America

Edited by Chris Roerden

First edition October 1997

10 9 8 7 6 5 4 3 2 1

Cataloging-in-Publication Data

Groetsch, Michael, 1949—

He promised he'd stop : helping women find safe passage from abusive relationships / Michael Groetsch.

p. cm.

Includes index.
ISBN 0-9651733-3-X (alk. paper)
1. Abused women – United States.   2. Abused women – United States – Life skills guides.   3. Family violence – United States.   I. Title.
HV 1445   1997
362.8'2'92 – dc21   97-69063

To my wife, Barbara, and my sons
Joshua, Jeremey, Gene, and Justin,
who have brought me a sense of oneness.
To my parents, Ewald and Johnteen,
who gave me my values.
To the memory of my late cousin, Kenny.
To Robin, wherever she may be.

Domestic violence is the leading cause of injury to women in the United States.

A woman is nine times more likely to be violently attacked in her own home than on the streets.

Contents

Acknowledgments

I would like to express my deepest gratitude to all who assisted me in bringing this book to its conclusion. Without their friendship, support, and technical assistance, *He Promised He'd Stop: Helping Women Find Safe Passage from Abusive Relationships* would not be a reality.

Foremost on my list are my wife, Barbara, and my sons, Joshua, Jeremey, Gene, and Justin. Not only have they tolerated my obsession with the batterer, but also their unwavering belief and encouragement that this book would be published were factors in its completion. In addition, Joshua's meticulous assistance in the completion of the final draft of the manuscript, even at the expense of his social life, will always be remembered.

I would also like to thank those friends and professionals who allowed me to share my knowledge with them in their respective areas of expertise. Judge John Shea of New Orleans Municipal Court, a man of integrity and morals, should be recognized as a pioneer in the issue of spousal abuse. The policies and procedures that he developed and allowed me to implement in his court since 1976 have become a model for the rest of our nation's judiciary. While his early efforts to concentrate on crimes of spousal abuse were often met with resistance and opposition, the dissenters now address him with respect and praise.

I will always value the friendship and support provided to me by Dr. Ciro Juarez-Nuñez. The wisdom he shared with me in my quest to understand the batterer has contributed heavily to my knowledge of a man that few understand.

Dr. Halina Margan, an adjunct professor at Tulane University School of Social Work, is also to be recognized for allowing me to share my insights of the batterer with her students over the last decade. While my concepts may clinically challenge the ideologies of some professionals in the field of social work, she has always afforded me the opportunity to present to her students philosophical perspectives that are so essential to academic growth.

Thanks are particularly in order to Chris Roerden and Sandra Christensen, whose creativity and editing skills transformed a somewhat complex topic into one that is very user friendly.

I will forever hold close to my heart the endless stream of trusting women who have walked through my doors to openly share their most intimate stories and fears. I only hope that this book provides to them the wisdom and identity that they have given to me.

Finally, I will always be grateful to the staff of the Crisis Prevention Institute for bringing this book and its related video training programs and seminars to the public.

Michael Groetsch

PART I

HE PROMISED HE'D STOP

Chapter 1

Who Are These Men?

We were college students on our first date together—a downtown movie and a friendly discussion of it over pasta at a nearby restaurant. When I drove Robin home that night, I sensed we were being followed. A red Corvette began tailgating us, its bright lights bouncing off my rearview mirror. Suddenly the driver sped up and pulled alongside, yelling obscenities at us. Robin cowered in the passenger seat. "He's my ex-boyfriend," she whispered. She warned me he was violent and always carried a gun.

That's when I realized we were in danger. But as an 18-year-old in the era of the sixties, I couldn't imagine how much.

As I drove into Robin's neighborhood, the Corvette pursued aggressively. I made no attempt to lose it, fearing that such a response would only provoke trouble. Instead, I tried to gather my thoughts and plan what to do once we reached my date's house. But I had no experience with such men.

Taking a deep breath, I pulled into the driveway. The Corvette pulled in directly behind me and blocked my exit. Before either of us could react, the passenger door flew open and Robin was pulled out of the car. Her ex-boyfriend began punching her in the face, and as she fell to the ground, he stomped and kicked her with both feet. The sound I heard was sickening—as if her bones were being crushed.

Though I quickly jumped across the seat to the open door to assist her, I was instantly met by the butt of a gun and forced back into the car. I retreated behind the steering wheel. The enraged boyfriend leaned in, holding the gun to my right temple. He was sweating profusely and crying hysterically. Cocking the hammer, he yelled, "I'm going to kill you."

At that moment I was convinced he would.

Despite all the noise and screaming, no one came to our aid—no one from Robin's house, no neighbors, no police. We were on our own. Somehow I tried negotiating with the attacker, as did Robin, who was lying on the ground outside the car. But he kept calling her a whore and claiming we were sleeping together. Each time I tried to assure him we'd never dated before that night, he became more enraged, demanding a confession and curling his index finger around the trigger. Twice during his tantrums, his finger tightened and he nearly fired the gun.

What lasted 10 or 15 minutes seemed like an hour. Gradually, his threats turned into a series of semi-apologies and pleadings: If I left and never looked back, he would let me go. He didn't have to bargain further. I assured him I wouldn't call the police or date Robin ever again. It was at that point his crying and sobbing stopped. He finally had what he wanted: control.

I never learned what happened to Robin. I do know she withdrew from the university. I didn't call the police. I was only 18 years old. I didn't want to be a dead hero.

Forgetting bad memories

Recently I was asked why I had gotten into my line of work as a probation officer for men who batter women. Did I grow up in a home with a violent father? No, I replied. Had I ever been directly victimized? No, I replied again—or so my memory convinced me.

But after thinking over the question for some time, I remembered the terrifying experience I'd had as a student some 30 years earlier. To my astonishment, I had forgotten it. I'd buried the memory, not wanting to recall it.

Often, a woman who is beaten by her husband or boyfriend similarly buries such memories, even when her nightmare of violence occurred more recently.

Like a month ago. Or last night.

If you are that woman, no one can blame you for wanting to forget such terror—or for trying to excuse the violence by telling yourself and others, "He had a good reason." No one can blame you for wanting to believe the attack never actually took place.

Disbelief is an understandable reaction.

It's hard to understand how a man who claims undying love is capable of savagely punching, biting, and humiliating the object of his love. It's hard to understand how a man who tearfully begs forgiveness and promises he'll stop his abuse can carry out his savagery over and over again.

These behaviors contradict each other. And to believe in a contradiction makes no sense. We *want* to believe that such vastly different behaviors will end and normalcy will return. We want to have hope that change will occur.

What drives a man to commit atrocities and acts of violence against the woman he says he loves? More important, how can you or I tell if the man is likely to repeat the violence? Maybe he won't repeat it; maybe he will.

Some men can learn to change their behavior; others cannot. The difference is crucial.

Is there a way to tell what that difference is?

If we don't know there's any difference among the kinds of men who beat women, the next beating could be a fatal one.

Every six hours a woman is murdered by her husband or boyfriend.

How can you be sure you will not become another shocking FBI statistic?

Mistakes about batterers

Before we try to understand *why* a man would beat the woman he claims to love, we need to recognize that all abusers are not the same.

Family and friends who try to help the woman end the violence in her life wrongly assume that all men abuse women for the same reasons. It's a serious error to believe that all abusers think alike or act alike.

Even some professionals make this error.

To assume that batterers are all the same can lead to poor judgment in dealing with the batterer. Poor judgment leads to poor decisions about how to change the situation—which often opens the door for further violence.

Good decisions can prevent further violence.

No single profile explains a batterer's violence, behaviors, and potential for change. It's a mistake to treat a battering male as if he had the same personality profile as every other batterer. Unfortunately, in most cases, the "one size fits all" approach is standard.

That's why it's important to distinguish among different types of batterers.

Each type exhibits a unique set of behaviors and character traits. Moreover, each type is capable of a different degree of violence. As a result, the risks to the victims of these abusive men are vastly different.

Different types of batterers

The issues are very complex, but there is a fairly simple way for us to talk about the different types of men.

1. To begin, picture a straight line made up of all the men who beat and batter their wives or girlfriends in the United States *in a single year.* Using the most conservative estimates of the number of batterers, if these men stood side by side, the line would reach from Washington, D.C., to Omaha, Nebraska.

> Tragically, the number of women who are beaten every year is at least 2 million. It might be as many as 10 million. The reason these numbers are so far apart is that for every case reported, an estimated 10 to 20 cases go unreported.

2. The next step in finding a way to discuss the different types of batterers is to imagine that we've been able to take this very long line of batterers and arrange them from "most dangerous" to "least dangerous."

At the extreme left end of the line are the batterers whose violence represents the least danger to their victims. Note that I did not say "no danger."

All battering is dangerous.

But for the purpose of distinguishing among all types of batterers, these are men who are *least likely* to inflict serious or lasting injury during an attack on a woman.

At the extreme right end of the line are the batterers who represent the greatest danger. The victims of these men are *most likely* to be very seriously hurt and even killed.

The type of line I'm describing is known as a *continuum.* In this particular continuum, each individual batterer represents one point along its length. All the points taken together make up the *Batterer's Continuum.*

The Batterer's Continuum

Even though we can talk about all batterers being lined up in this manner does not mean that any one individual will actually behave in a predictable way.

Individuals are more complex than that.

The Batterer's Continuum is simply a device to help us describe the similarities and differences among the various types of batterers.

THE BATTERER'S CONTINUUM

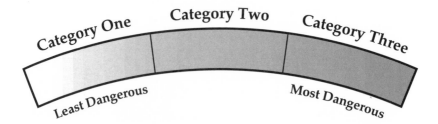

The Batterer's Continuum can be divided into any number of separate groups. My work with batterers has shown me that it's useful to identify these men as falling into three groups.

For convenience, we call these groups of men Category 1, Category 2, and Category 3 batterers.

- Category 1 represents the man whose violent behavior poses the least danger. I discuss his type in the next chapter.
- Category 3 represents the most dangerous abuser. We take a look at his capacity for violence in Chapters 3 and 4.
- Category 2 is made up of batterers who lie somewhere in between these two extremes. I introduce their behaviors in Chapter 5.

Now that you know how the Batterer's Continuum works and why it's important to be able to identify the different types of batterers, here's a list of some of the major factors I've taken into account in putting it together.

THE BATTERER'S CONTINUUM

CATEGORY 1	CATEGORY 2	CATEGORY 3
Least Dangerous	**Moderately Dangerous**	**Very Dangerous**
1. A normal male in abnormal circumstances	1. A male with several character defects	1. A male with a personality disorder
2. Abuse is situational, isolated	2. Abuse is neither isolated nor ongoing; it's sporadic	2. Abuse is ongoing, systematic; shows a chronic pattern
3. Cause of aggression: 90% external 10% internal	3. Cause of aggression: 50% external 50% internal	3. Cause of aggression: 10% external 90% internal
4. Previous relationships with women were not violent	4. Some previous relationships with women were violent	4. All previous relationships with women were violent
5. No premarital abuse	5. Some premarital abuse	5. Frequent premarital abuse
6. No use of weapons	6. Some use of weapons	6. Frequent use of weapons
7. Feels genuine remorse	7. Feels limited remorse	7. Feels no remorse; has no conscience
8. Very treatable	8. Might be treatable	8. Not treatable

Summary

- It's understandable that a woman will try to forget that she is being abused by a man who insists he loves her and begs for forgiveness. She will find excuses for his behavior and even deny that she is being beaten.
- Some men can learn to change their behavior; others cannot. The difference is crucial.
- All abusers are not the same. It's a serious mistake to deal with abusers as if they shared the same personality profile.

- The likelihood of serious and permanent harm to the woman who is beaten varies, depending on the type of batterer. Regardless, *all* abuse is potentially dangerous.
- The Batterer's Continuum is a tool to help us look at the different types of men who batter so we can describe their similarities and differences.
- It is useful to look at three categories of batterers, because that helps us distinguish those batterers who can learn to change from those who are beyond rehabilitation. The difference can prevent grave injury and even save lives.

Chapter 2

Category 1: The Remorseful Batterer

John was a loving husband and father, and he got along reasonably well with most people. One day his little boy came home from school and said, "Dad, let's go out and play." John answered, "I don't have time right now, but you go on out and I'll be there in a little while."

So the child went outside alone. Five minutes later he was hit by a car. John ran out, picked up the boy, and watched helplessly as his child died in his arms. He was overwhelmed with unbearable pain, anger, and guilt. Several weeks later during a minor disagreement with his wife, his emotions spilled over and he hit her.

In the ten years they'd been married, he had never before hit his wife.

Recognizing the type

John is an example of a Category 1 batterer.
- He has no history of abusing a woman.
- His victim is not at great risk of being seriously injured or killed.
- His physical aggression follows a catastrophic external event.

BATTERER'S CONTINUUM

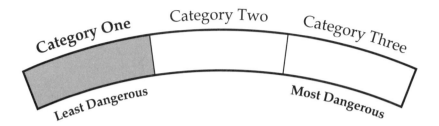

Of the three types of batterers, this category, Category 1, is the least dangerous.

But please keep this in mind:

Any episode of violence is dangerous.

No history of violence

- He has no history of beating his wife, either before or after they were married.
- He has no history of abusing women in other intimate relationships.
- His physical aggression is usually limited to one or two episodes.
- His violence occurs over a specific and limited period of time—usually weeks or months, not years.
- His aggression is not likely to be repeated in the future.

Least dangerous

The Category 1 batterer inflicts injuries that are usually less severe than those inflicted on the wives and girlfriends of abusers in Categories 2 and 3.

This doesn't mean the injuries cannot become crippling or fatal—it means permanent disability or death is much less likely with a Category 1 batterer.

- He is able to control his impulses fairly well.
- He has no pattern of beating his partner when she is pregnant.
- He tends not to use weapons.
- He does not torture his victim or seek to mutilate or disfigure her.
- His assaults are not premeditated but are spontaneous and without malice. He does not consciously intend to harm or injure his victim.

Moreover, he does not regularly experience irrational outbursts, temper tantrums, or extreme jealousy. In general he is not overly suspicious, cruel, or suicidal.

This doesn't mean that a Category 1 batterer is a terrific person with no faults or character defects.

It's just that he doesn't have so many of them that he presents an ongoing problem. If he did, he'd be classified as a Category 2 or 3 batterer.

What provokes him

Several additional signs are also important in identifying the Category 1 batterer:

- His violence tends to be isolated, not part of a pattern of physically abusing women.
- His violence is an extreme reaction directly related to some catastrophic event in his life, such as the loss of:
  - » a job
  - » a significant amount of money
  - » a friend
  - » a loved one
- His violence begins shortly after he experiences such a loss or other trauma. It might also be related to:
  - » drug or alcohol abuse
  - » extreme stress
  - » anxiety
  - » depression

I am *not* saying that extreme grief or guilt or *any other emotion* excuses the violence.

No one has the right to strike another person for any reason.

What I *am* saying is that men whose physical violence falls in the least dangerous category of the Batterer's Continuum—Category 1—are usually reacting in extreme ways to isolated events in their lives.

Poor coping skills

People differ widely in being able to handle the problems that life throws into their paths. They have not learned how to deal appropriately with difficulties. They are said to have *poor coping skills.*

Men with poor coping skills are most likely to become Category 1 batterers.

In general, this type of batterer is a fairly normal male who is unable to handle abnormal events or situations.

He reacts with extreme emotion to circumstances that he feels are beyond his control.

When these circumstances are eliminated or when the stress is reduced, the physical abuse, in most cases, stops.

Motivated by conscience

The Category 1 batterer seldom comes to the attention of the criminal justice system.

Only a very small number of the cases of wife beating that come into court fit the profile of the Category 1 batterer. Of the men who become known to the police, this batterer is most affected by his brush with the law. That's because he is far more motivated to avoid a police record than to continue hurting his victim.

Studies indicate that arresting and prosecuting woman-beaters reduces domestic violence.

If the Category 1 batterer does encounter the law, he is the type of man most likely to change his behavior.

That's because:

- He is better able to control his impulses.
- He feels guilt and genuine *remorse* for his aggressive behavior.
- He cares about his victim's feelings—not just his own feelings.
- He is able to bond with other people—a quality known as *empathy*.

It's this quality of bonding or *empathizing with others*, together with his ability to *feel remorse*, that distinguishes the Category 1 batterer from other men who physically abuse women.

That's why I refer to the Category 1 batterer as the *Remorseful Batterer*.

Of course, like all men who batter women, the Remorseful Batterer may try to minimize or "play down" the seriousness of his behavior. He may also excuse or *rationalize* his behavior, saying to himself and others: "I had a good reason."

But the Remorseful Batterer excuses and rationalizes his behavior much less than any other type of batterer. He usually has a keen sense of responsibility for his actions.

Motivated to change

In addition, the Remorseful Batterer is the most likely type of batterer to seek help for his problems on his own, without being pressured by others to do so. Often, he seeks help *before* coming to the attention of the authorities.

He is the most frequent type of batterer to seek out a therapist or counselor to help him.

Because he feels remorse, empathy, and guilt for the wrong he has done, he is motivated to change so he won't repeat his destructive behavior.

In working with a counselor, he usually shows a good deal of *insight* about himself.

That means he is able to:

- understand why he behaves abusively
- express his feelings and emotions
- show love and caring
- develop healthy relationships with others that are based on respect and mutual concern.

These are good signs.

They indicate that the Remorseful Batterer is an excellent candidate for professional counseling, such as *psychotherapy*.

When this man shows an interest in getting treatment to help him change his behavior, the decision is one that family, friends, and others can support wholeheartedly.

Counseling can make a real difference for this type of batterer.

- It can help him learn healthier ways of dealing with situations in which he feels he has no control.
- It can also help his wife or girlfriend end the fear of further violence.

I want to emphasize that the Remorseful Batterer has this ability to change because he is a relatively normal human being—except for the aggression that erupts when he fails to cope.

Although the moral character of the Remorseful Batterer is not necessarily beyond criticism, he is usually a law-abiding citizen who is non-threatening and non-abusive in his social and interpersonal relationships.

He is usually employed, and others view him as a good husband, father, and provider.

In the absence of unusually stressful situations, he functions no differently than the average male does.

In fact—although this is not a pleasant thought—many males, given the wrong set of external circumstances, are probably capable of Category 1 abuse.

Summary

- Of the three types of males who physically abuse women, the Category 1 or Remorseful Batterer is the least likely to seriously injure or kill his victim.
- He does not tend to use weapons, torture or disfigure his victim, or consciously intend to harm or injure her. Rather, his assaults are spontaneous and without malice.
- His violence is limited to a few specific episodes and is not likely to occur again.
- These episodes are related to an external event, such as a major loss, for which he lacks appropriate coping skills.
- His ability to feel remorse and to bond or empathize with others distinguishes him from the more dangerous categories of abusers.
- He is the type of abuser most likely to seek help in dealing with his problems and learning to change.
- The Remorseful Batterer is a very likely candidate for rehabilitation.

Chapter 3

Category 3:
The Serial Batterer

One day in 1990, in a small town near Grand Forks, North Dakota, a man shot and killed his wife. He also shot and killed his 11-year-old daughter, and then himself.

On the same day in a small southern Illinois city across the river from St. Louis, Missouri, a man armed with a handgun shot and killed his wife, their daughter, and their one-year-old grandson. He set the house on fire and shot at the firefighters who came to the scene. Then, by staying in his burning home, he ended his own life.

Also on the same day, in Spanaway, Washington, a third man smashed through a sliding glass door to shoot and kill his ex-wife and her new husband. He also shot and killed his six-year-old daughter and his 14-year-old daughter.

In a single 24-hour period, these episodes of domestic violence wiped out 12 members of three families. Though these were not the only murders of an intimate partner occurring that day, they were among the more violent.

Each murderer is an example of a Category 3 batterer.

These 12 deaths show the kind of violence this batterer is capable of committing. Each murder shows the extreme danger such a man poses not only to his partner, but also to her family, to friends, and even to his own children.

An FBI report from 1993 shows a shocking statistic: 29 percent of all women murdered in the United States are murdered by their current or former husbands and boyfriends.

There is no way to know how many more women are tortured or mutilated by their partners, or die from internal injuries they receive over many years of brutal beatings. The number, I am certain, is in the millions.

Recognizing the type

The Category 3 batterer is at the extreme opposite end of the Batterer's Continuum from the Category 1 batterer.

BATTERER'S CONTINUUM

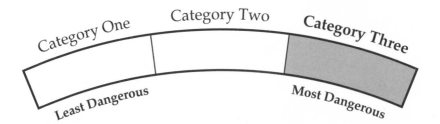

Of the three types of batterers, this man is the most dangerous.
- He has a history of abusing women.
- His victim has the *highest* risk of being seriously injured or killed.
- His physical aggression comes from somewhere inside himself rather than from some major event taking place in his life.

If such a man is your partner, you are constantly in danger of injury, mutilation, and death.

Not all Category 3 batterers commit murder, but they all have the *potential* for doing so.

History of violence

A closer look reveals that the Category 3 batterer is a *Serial Batterer:*

- He has abused many women over much of his lifetime. It's likely that *all* his relationships with women have been violent.
- He beat his wife before they were married.
- He batters on an ongoing basis. Many victims say they have trouble remembering when one beating ends and the next begins.
- His aggression is absolutely certain to continue.

Serial Batterers are no more able to change their behavior than serial rapists and serial killers are able to change theirs.

Such violence is not limited to partners who have known each other a long time.

One woman reported that her husband deliberately broke her arm on their honeymoon.

Another told how her husband gave her a black eye on their first date.

Each man excused his attack by saying he'd had too much to drink. Yet each victim reported that within two years of marriage, she was being physically abused at least five times a month.

Sometimes a woman thinks the abuse that occurs while the couple is dating will stop after they get married. But it is much more likely that it will continue.

In fact, odds are that the abuse and violence will greatly *increase.*

During a court hearing, one woman testified to being aware that the man she married had been arrested for stabbing two of his former girlfriends, and that he had beaten his first wife to death. She was worried about her personal safety, and about his future victims.

Any woman who is thinking about a relationship with a man who has a history of violence should consider that history in predicting the future. The probability of his beating her as he did his former lovers is nearly 100 percent!

Extremely dangerous

If you glance at any local newspaper on any day, you'll see endless reports of the terrible violence and aggression caused by Serial Batterers. These news reports are vivid reminders of the gruesome and perverse acts of torture, mutilation, and murder some men can inflict on the women they say they love.

- Very often, the woman is permanently disabled or disfigured by her partner.
- According to FBI statistics, every six hours in the United States, a woman is killed by her partner.

Most of the damage does not make news.

- Not reported is the woman's pain—physical and emotional—which is indescribable.
- Not reported is her extreme and ongoing stress, which is likely to lower her resistance to disease.
- In addition, an untold number of deaths, disabilities, and diseases are not even *identified* as being the result of long-term physical abuse, which can cause internal physical damage. Each assault not only creates new injuries, but also worsens old injuries.

A body that's repeatedly battered has a much harder time repairing itself.

A batterer can cause his victim to suffer from:
- » blood clots, which could cause strokes
- » damage to the neck and spinal cord
- » ulcers
- » loss of memory
- » venereal disease
- » vision problems
- » hearing loss
- » intense chronic headaches
- » high blood pressure and heart disease

Newspaper stories usually tell of a man who is ruthless, intensely cold, and without remorse. One newspaper told of an especially grisly murder in which the batterer killed his victim and then cut her arms, legs, and head off her lifeless body.

I am not telling you these facts because I enjoy shocking you. On the contrary. I am very concerned that if you—and millions of other women like you—have a man in your life who fits the description of a Category 3 Serial Batterer, you could be in great danger, far greater than you realize.

No woman deserves to live in such danger. No one deserves to be the victim of such violence—EVER—for any reason.

Unfortunately, the crime of domestic violence is so common that many people get used to hearing about it. They become insensitive to the horror of it. Sometimes, the victim's family and friends become numb to the pain and terror she experiences.

Even the words "domestic violence" sound impersonal. The words no longer alarm people to the awful reality of what is taking place in the privacy of so many homes.

But for the woman herself, and often for her children, as well, the ongoing danger, pain, and terror are very real.

Behaves brutally

If you are the victim of such violence, you might recognize that the man in your life fits the description of the Category 3 Serial Batterer. Such men are found in every social class, every income level, and every suburb, city, and small town.

To help you recognize this dangerous batterer, here are some other characteristics of his brutal behavior.

He routinely beats his partner, bruising her body and breaking her bones. In an alarmingly high number of these attacks, he permanently injures, disfigures, and disables her.

Although most of these abusers do not murder their victims, all Serial Batterers are potential killers.

The Serial Batterer often reveals a pattern of abuse:
- He beats his partner when she is pregnant.
- He tends to use weapons.
- He systematically tortures his victim or mutilates and disfigures her.
- Some of his assaults may be spontaneous, but often they are premeditated and malicious.

The Serial Batterer deliberately sets out to injure his victim.

He wants to dominate and control his partner, and he uses many different behaviors to frighten her.

He counts on controlling her through fear.

Often, he threatens to kill her, the children, and even himself. If he owns a gun he tells her he will use it on her if necessary. He might fire the gun inside the house, sometimes shooting dangerously close to his victim.

One woman testified that her husband shot the phone off the wall with a .38 caliber pistol because she refused to hang up as he demanded.

Another woman said that during her husband's rage, he held a loaded gun to her head and to the head of her four-year-old son.

Some men are known to cut the clothes of their victims with knives and threaten to do the same to their bodies.

Threats of burning the house and setting the woman on fire with gasoline are reported surprisingly often.

Usually, her car is vandalized, furniture destroyed, windows shattered, and doors smashed.

Often, these violent tirades involve unthinkable and inhuman acts of torture and mutilation. In one municipal court over a short period of time, numerous victims of abuse presented shocking testimony of such acts.

> *One victim told how her husband shoved the barrel of a loaded .38 revolver up her vagina and threatened to shoot if she refused to have sex with him.*
>
> *Similar testimony came from a woman who was rushed to a hospital after her boyfriend had taken the splintered end of a broken stick and forced it up her rectum.*
>
> *Another victim reported she was held down while her boyfriend pushed a hot curling iron to her face and body. She is permanently scarred and disfigured over about 25 percent of her body.*
>
> *A woman painfully testified that her husband had attacked her with a set of nunchucks (two sticks joined by a chain), almost severing her vocal cords. He completed his attack by scalping her forehead with a rusty knife.*
>
> *One battered woman showed hideous scars on her arms, legs, neck, and face. She said the scars were caused by her boyfriend, who viciously bit her during his attacks. In many of his assaults, he ripped flesh from her body with his teeth.*

The stories are endless, and so is the number of victims.

Is emotionally abusive

The aggression of a Serial Batterer is not limited to physical violence alone. He often uses emotional and psychological abuse to terrify her and get her completely under his control. For example:

- He ridicules her and puts her down, in private and in public, in front of friends and family. He relentlessly destroys her self-esteem and fills her with feelings of worthlessness and shame.
- He manipulates her by promising what he knows she wants to hear, but only until he gets what he wants.
- He is dangerously jealous, not only of any man his wife or girlfriend may interact with, but also of members of her family, friends, and even his own children.
- He tries to cut her off from her family, friends, and the rest of the world. He wants her to feel isolated.
- He dominates her in every way, controlling her actions and the words she speaks. He even tries to control her thoughts, and over a long enough period of time he succeeds.

By repeatedly humiliating his victim, he takes away any sense of self-worth she has.

- He insists that she is ugly, stupid, a poor mother and wife, and unworthy of family and friends.
- When she expresses an opinion, he publicly orders her to shut up, saying her ideas and thoughts are useless.
- When she cooks and does housework, he tells her she's a rotten housekeeper.
- If she attempts to bring in more money for her family by getting a job, he tells her no employer would ever want her, and he orders her to stop looking for work.

In his efforts to cut off his victim from anything beyond his immediate interests, he not only forbids her to work outside the home but also stops her from making new friends.

He also demands that she give up the friendships and relationships she already has. He punishes her for any signs of independence.

Often, he won't allow her to speak or visit with her friends, parents, or brothers and sisters. He tells her these people are "bad for her," and it's "in her best interests" not to talk to them or see them. He may take the car keys to stop her from visiting them. If she disobeys him, he intimidates her with insults and beats her with his fists or anything else he can lay his hands on.

When he beats her, he batters her face in a deliberate attempt to destroy her appearance.

Even in their sexual relationship, he tries to make her feel guilty for not having sex when he demands it. When she gives in, he performs perverted acts to further humiliate her.

Wants absolute control

As a result of repeated abuse—emotional, psychological, and physical—the partner of a Serial Batterer becomes brainwashed in the same way that a prisoner of war is brainwashed.

She is no longer his girlfriend or his wife. She is his hostage.

The Serial Batterer is very aware of his attempts to destroy his partner's self-esteem and her emotional support.

He is very aware of wanting to erase her sense of herself as a separate person.

He wants her to become clay in his hands. And whether she knows it or not, she begins to change into whatever shape he desires—just like a lump of clay that he manipulates.

It's a shape he can totally control:
- through the deliberate use of humiliation, shame, and isolation from others
- through the constant fear of being brutally attacked and tortured
- through the frequent threats of "I'll kill you!"

By means of these tactics, the Serial Batterer attempts to control his partner's sense of her own identity as a separate person. Using fear, torture, and humiliation, he tries to wipe out her individuality and absorb her sense of her own personal identity into his.

Her personality, her sense of herself, and everything that goes into making up her personal identity—he wants all of it to become his.

He wants her to be without any free will of her own and to relate to everything through him.

Like a brainwashed prisoner of war, she will eventually become an empty shell and ultimately lose her ability to think for herself.

She is being trained not to have feelings or to act on them. Instead, her abuser will think for her, feel for her, and act for her.

Eventually, the batterer succeeds in getting her to relate to herself—as well as to the world around her—through him alone.

His victim's need to escape

It is not easy for the victim of a Serial Batterer to escape. Through his relentless and deliberate manipulation of her, she comes to agree with his view of her and to accept his treatment of her.

Although his view of her is not an accurate one, her ability to judge for herself is destroyed.

Because her sense of self is so weakened by his abuse, she has little expectation of a better life for herself. Without any expectations or hope, she has no dream or vision to help motivate her to get out of her private hell.

In addition, she is too afraid to leave.

Nevertheless:

To stop being the victim of abuse by a Serial Batterer, she has to leave.

> **If you are the wife or girlfriend of a Serial Batterer, leaving may be difficult for you, but it's essential to saving your life.**
> **You need to:**
> **1. Get a safety plan.**
> **2. Get out.**

Chapter 12 tells you how to safely leave your violent batterer.

Takes no responsibility

Here's how this type of abuser behaves when he comes into contact with professionals, especially those who represent the criminal justice system or who run rehabilitation or treatment programs:

- He denies responsibility for his behavior.
- He blames the victim or others for his actions.
- At times he denies that the violence even took place.
- He minimizes his behavior, downplaying the seriousness of his victim's injuries even when confronted with evidence of how severe those injuries are.
- He finds excuses to justify his violence, blaming the woman or "circumstances beyond his control."
- He is virtually impossible to rehabilitate.

Remember when I talked about the mistake people make in thinking all abusers are the same? I pointed out that even professionals make this mistake.

Not every batterer can change, and it's dangerous to believe he can.

Batterers who fit the profile of the Category 1 Remorseful Batterer make good candidates for counseling and rehabilitation. Others do not.

Until each Serial Batterer is accurately identified and brought to justice for his crimes of violence, the only way for a woman to end the cycle of her abuse is to leave him.

When his victim leaves

In the next few pages I describe how the Serial Batterer usually behaves once he discovers that his wife or girlfriend has left. The information is bound to add to her fear of leaving, but I feel it's important for her and her family and friends to know what to expect.

In spite of her fear, I urge a woman in a relationship with a Serial Batterer to get out. With the proper precautions, she *can* avoid the violence that follows her leaving.

If she stays, she will continue being terrorized, injured beyond healing, and brainwashed beyond recognition.

So far, we've been looking at a few of the violent behaviors that occur while the Serial Batterer and his victim are still together. Once she leaves, her situation is likely to get worse—unless she has an effective safety plan in place.

Her abuser uses almost any method to get her back.

- He begs desperately for her return, harassing her with mail and phone calls.
- He tries to intimidate her verbally and physically, stalking her at home and at work.
- He destroys her property.
- He threatens her safety and the safety of her family and friends. He may even kidnap her children to force her to return to him.

The Category 3 Serial Batterer hunts his former partner in the same manner a wolf hunts its prey.

He follows and stalks her in the shadows of night. When he attacks, he tells her if she doesn't return, he'll kill her.

If she parks and leaves her car, he slashes her tires, cuts the wires under the hood, throws acid on the paint, and takes a hammer or brick to the windows.

One woman who tried to get away from her former husband discovered he had used a blowtorch to burn the inside of her new car. He left a note attached to the burned-out car saying she was next.

Another woman caught her husband in the act of using a sledgehammer on her car. The police were called, but they said they couldn't arrest him for destroying the car because the title to the car was in both their names. After the police left, her husband beat her with the sledgehammer for having called them.

If the woman refuses to get back together with her abuser, he calls her on the phone over and over again, one moment hysterically begging her to come back, the next moment threatening her with physical harm if she doesn't.

Although he puts notes under her door insisting that he loves her, he turns violent if she doesn't return.

If she's employed, he harasses her on her job and stalks her as she leaves work.

One man managed to stalk his girlfriend while he was in jail for an earlier attack on her. Allegedly, he had his sister and a couple of friends wait for her as she left work and throw acid in her face. Right after this cruel attack, he called her from jail to say that he'd ordered the attack and that he still loved her.

Nothing is more terrifying for a woman who has left a battering husband than to have him come crashing through her windows or doors in the middle of the night. As she sleeps in the darkness of her bedroom, this man defuses the electrical box, cuts the telephone wires, and breaks windows or doors to get inside her house. He is often armed. Even if she doesn't resist his demands, he deliberately destroys her property and beats her up.

When he's ready to go, he leaves the terrible memory of his violence behind him, sometimes kidnapping her children and threatening to keep them or hurt them if she doesn't return to him.

The trauma she and her children experience is beyond words.

Terror paralyzes her emotionally and physically as she lies in bed in a state of sleepless watchfulness. She does not know when or how he will strike.

What is certain is that he will strike.

Evelyn described how her ex-husband always came looking for her each time he finished serving time for violating a restraining order.

"I learned to lie in bed at night with my children in anticipation of his arrival. We would even sleep with our shoes on," she said. "One night he came crashing through my bedroom window. He didn't even try to open it. He simply stood on a fence and hurled his body through the glass. As he lay on the floor trying to regain his balance, I grabbed the phone to call the police, but he'd already cut the wires from outside. I grabbed the kids and ran, screaming for help. As we stumbled through the darkened house, he came after us with a hammer. By the time we made it to the back door, the police arrived." Her neighbor had called 911.

That was the last time Evelyn saw her ex-husband. "I always felt that he would commit suicide, but that he'd probably kill the children and me first," she said. While driving across a bridge with his mother, he jumped from the passenger seat and hurled his body across the rail, falling 200 feet to the ground.

"I guess I should have felt bad, but I didn't. I felt relieved. For the first time, my children and I could live and sleep in peace. But even though he's dead, my children often clutch me at night as if they still anticipate his arrival."

No matter what methods he uses, the Serial Batterer tries to put fear into the soul of his victim. He usually succeeds.

Fear can be so crippling that many women who think about pulling out of abusive relationships find themselves too afraid to do so, painfully aware of what could happen.

When Vonelle finally decided to move to another city to get away from further abuse, she had trouble deciding whether to slip out when her abuser was not watching, or to tell him the exact time she was leaving. She finally decided that to slip out was more risky. Later, she explained her reasoning:

"When he finds out I lied, he will hunt me down, find me, and kill me. But if I tell him the truth, even though he might try to prevent my leaving, his rage will not be as intense, and perhaps my life will be spared."

Targets of rage

His wife or girlfriend is not the only one in danger from the Serial Batterer. He is a threat to anyone he thinks is trespassing on his turf. He thinks of his mate as something he owns, something he has clear property rights to.

He resents anyone who gets in the way of his control over "his property."

When his victim is trying to escape, the people who try to help her can also become targets of his unpredictable rage and aggression. This includes attorneys and anyone who helps her enforce her legal rights. It includes doctors and therapists who treat her, and social workers who try to help her get a job or find day care for her children.

Those most at risk are her relatives and the friends who give her and her children a place to stay.

Ted stormed into the home of his ex-girlfriend. As her family and friends sat at the dinner table frozen with fear, he opened fire with a .22 caliber rifle and blasted them one after another. In all, he murdered five people— his girlfriend, her mother and stepfather, her new boyfriend, and her four-year-old child.

We don't know exactly how often the Serial Batterer attacks the friends and family of his estranged partner. We just know that it happens all too often.

Because of this risk, it is *absolutely necessary* for relatives, friends, and other people connected to the victim to realize the danger they may be in. It's essential that all of them work out a plan to defend themselves, both physically and legally.

> **PLAN OF DEFENSE**
>
> **A wise plan of defense includes:**
> 1. **having an understanding of the batterer's personality and how he behaves**
> 2. **setting up a strong safety plan (described in Chapter 12)**
> 3. **being alert to danger and very, very watchful.**

Helping a victim of a Serial Batterer without having a plan places everyone at great risk.

I'm not suggesting that professionals, relatives, and friends should abandon the woman who is in a relationship with such a batterer.

Without help, the woman and her children have little hope of escaping the web of violence they are trapped in.

I am also not saying that the batterer will always harm, injure, or kill people who get in the way of his relationship with his wife or girlfriend.

What I *am* saying is that the danger of becoming the target of the batterer's violence is always present. So everyone involved must be prepared with a practical *plan of safety.*

Personality disorders

The Serial Batterer has serious emotional problems.

He has an extremely unstable personality, which is generally referred to as a personality disorder.

- He is unable to truly love another person.
- He is cold. He has no conscience, no sympathy for his victim, no guilt. He feels no remorse.

- He does not bond with anyone, a quality known as *empathy*. He does not relate to the feelings of others. Nonetheless, he may be a very emotionally intense person, and he may even seem to be an exciting person.
- His self-esteem is extremely low, and he feels intensely inadequate, despite appearing to be self-confident, even arrogant.
- He is often obviously distressed. His moods change rapidly, going from one extreme to the other. He often shows signs of anxiety, anger, and depression.
- He may be unable to hold a job.
- He may have a criminal record.
- He usually abuses alcohol or drugs or both.
- He is unable to control his impulses.
- His behavior is generally inappropriate and frequently disgusting to those who interact with him.
- He has no insight into himself. He does not know why he batters, and he is not motivated to change. He is almost impossible to treat or rehabilitate.

These behaviors are signs of a severe personality disorder.

Not all men with personality disorders are batterers, but it's likely that almost all Serial Batterers have personality disorders.

What is it that causes a man to deliberately disfigure and disable the woman he claims to love? What type of man stalks his ex-partner in the same way an animal hunts its prey?

Usually, this man comes from a background in which emotional and physical violence were "normal." Often, his father battered his mother. Often, he himself was abused.

However, it is not my purpose to analyze whether or not a background of violence is the "cause" of this man's pounding his wife with a lead pipe while her children watch and scream with fear.

My purpose is to describe the behavior of this dangerous abuser so his victims will recognize how serious it is
and take action to protect themselves.

Too often, attempts to *explain* such behavior can end up
excusing it or *justifying* it—that is, making it seem okay. Violence is not okay. It cannot be excused.

Whatever the cause of this man's violence, there is *no*
excuse for his kicking and punching his wife in the stomach when she's pregnant. There is *no* justifying his mutilat-
ing his girlfriend's sexual organs.

Myths about battering

*One newspaper reported the complaint that a man's
wife wasn't spending enough "quality time" with him.
He killed her.*

This is an example of the batterer's blaming his victim.

It is also an example of the media's repeating the
batterer's complaint. When newspaper, radio, and TV reporters try to make sense of violence that is completely
senseless, they often use explanations given by the batterer. But in repeating the batterer's complaints, the media
add to the impression that such explanations are reasonable.

Sometimes reporters say that the murder of a wife or
girlfriend was "a crime of passion."

I believe the media do these victims a great injustice when
they suggest that such a man beats and kills the woman in
his life because of something *she* did to provoke him, or
because of other events such as financial problems or stress
at work.

These are excuses.

Those who offer such excuses badly misjudge the type
of man who is capable of extreme aggression. Not only the
media but also family and friends sometimes make the

mistake of blaming different events in the batterer's life for his crimes of violence.

Tragically, even police, judges, doctors, social workers, and others in the helping professions blame these events as well.

Here's one example of how a professional misjudged the seriousness of an act committed by a Serial Batterer:

> *A man walked into a department store where his estranged wife worked and shot her at point-blank range with a small caliber handgun. Later, when a reporter interviewed a therapist about the incident, this professional is reported to have said, "These men are choking on stress."*

All the stress in the world is no reason for a man to walk into a store and shoot his wife—or to commit *any* act of terror. That's just another excuse.

At some time in his life, every man in modern society can expect to have problems that are intensely stressful, even overwhelming: severe money problems, major job loss, or grief over the death of a loved one.

But no matter how bad things get, most men never physically abuse the women in their lives.

Most men *never* behave in the maliciously cruel manner of a Serial Batterer. No event or external situation has anything to do with the true reasons for the aggression of a seriously disturbed abuser.

I am not suggesting that stressful situations cannot *trigger* acts of anger and rage. Surely they can, as we saw in the example of violence committed by the Remorseful Batterer. However, the majority of men have some ability to control their violent impulses. They have some awareness of how wrong it is to seriously harm another person.

But the man who fits the description of the Serial Batterer has neither the ability to control his impulses nor concern that his behavior is wrong.

Although this individual's aggressive, violent actions can be *triggered* by outside stresses, it is not *caused* by them. He does not batter his girlfriend because he was laid off at work. He does not beat his wife because he lost money in the stock market. He does not hold a gun to his partner's head because she looked at another man or burnt the toast.

He offers these and a hundred other "reasons" solely to excuse or play down his brutality.

In reality, his brutality occurs because something is terribly wrong with his personality.

Inside him is an enormous amount of anger and continuous conflict. He's his own pressure cooker ready to explode at any moment.

His internal turmoil is very different from the anger that leads the Remorseful Batterer to strike out when overwhelmed by circumstances outside himself.

For the Serial Batterer, such "external" circumstances merely trigger what is already there.

He is a smoldering volcano of anger that never stops erupting. Like an active volcano, his angry violence is always just beneath the surface.

Summary

- Of the three types of batterers, the Category 3 or Serial Batterer is the most dangerous.
- Often, he uses a weapon, mutilates and permanently disfigures the woman he claims to love, terrorizes her and her children, and is capable of murdering her and anyone who gets in his way.
- He has a history of battering, and the likelihood of that violent history repeating itself in his future relationships is nearly 100 percent.
- He is no more able to change his behavior than serial rapists or serial killers are able to change theirs.
- No woman deserves to live in such danger.

- In addition to inflicting physical abuse, the Serial Batterer uses emotional and psychological abuse to dominate and control his victim. He ridicules and humiliates her and cuts her off from family and friends.
- He attempts to destroy her self-esteem and free will, brainwashing her until she can no longer think for herself. He wants her to relate to herself and to the world around her through him alone.
- Virtually the only way to end the cycle of abuse is for the woman to leave. A safety plan is essential to protect her and her family and friends from the violence that usually increases after she leaves.
- The Serial Batterer is nearly impossible to rehabilitate because he has very serious emotional problems. Those who try to explain the cause of his violence usually end up excusing or justifying it. Violence cannot be excused.
- The stress of events in his life might trigger his aggression but not cause it. Most men experience intensely stressful problems that never lead them to commit violent crimes.
- The Serial Batterer cannot control his aggressive impulses. Nor is he concerned by how his violence affects others. He has a serious personality disorder.

Chapter 4

Six Types of Serial Batterers

"It was not unusual for Al to stop at the liquor store after work, pick up a fifth of liquor, and begin drinking as soon as we got home. He usually went through at least a fifth a day, and most of the time would eat nothing. It's my opinion," writes Carrie, "that he used the drinking to 'let the genie out of the bottle'—in other words, to enable him to abuse me.

"Al would sit in his chair in front of the TV and drink until after I went to bed. By the time I'd fallen into a deep sleep, he would stomp into our bedroom yelling and screaming. Often, he'd grab the mattress and dump me off the bed onto the floor.

"Once when I was getting ready for bed," continued Carrie, "I went into the kitchen in my nightgown. As he screamed at me, he knocked me down, grabbed my ankles, pulled me upside down, and banged my head on the floor. This sort of thing happened with increasing regularity during the last four of the five years we were together."

Carrie calls it "the night terrors."

A psychiatrist would say that the Serial Batterer has a personality disorder.

We all know what disorder looks like. In a closet, disorder is a jumble and tangle of clothing. In a teenager's room, disorder is a mess. Think of a personality disorder as a mental mess, in which the difference between beliefs and reality is jumbled and tangled.

Cancer of the personality

A personality disorder can also be thought of as similar to a mental cancer. It eats into a person's sense of conscience and concern for others, and it destroys the social skills needed to interact with others.

Almost all Serial Batterers have personality disorders. This does not mean they are unaware of their behaviors.

Rarely is the Serial Batterer *psychotic* or out of touch with reality. Nor does his personality disorder qualify him for the legal posture of being "innocent by reason of insanity."

The fact is, the Serial Batterer frequently premeditates his violence. He beats his victim with the full intent of harming her. He knows and understands right from wrong. He knows exactly what he is doing and doesn't care.

If you have a man in your life who fits the description of a Serial Batterer, you are in great danger.

Psychiatrists have identified many kinds of personality disorders, each one characterized by a particular set of behaviors. When we look at these behaviors, we see that almost all Serial Batterers have personality disorders.

Although there are many types and combinations of personality disorders, six types show up again and again:
1. Narcissistic Personality Disorder
2. Antisocial Personality Disorder
3. Borderline Personality Disorder
4. Histrionic Personality Disorder
5. Paranoid Personality Disorder
6. Obsessive-Compulsive Personality Disorder.

To help you recognize the Category 3 or Serial Batterer, let's look at each of these disorders.

The Narcissistic Batterer

In ancient Greece, so the story goes, a young man named Narcissus was so handsome that when he saw his own reflection in a pool of water, he fell completely in love with it. In fact, he loved his own image so much that he was unable to tear himself away from it, and eventually he died of starvation.

Today, in describing someone who cares only about himself, and who is not interested in anyone or anything other than himself, we say:

- he is a *narcissist* (pronounced NAHR-si-SIST)
- his behavior is *narcissistic* (pronounced NAHR-si-SIS-tik).

This individual feels he is the most important person in the world.

Most Serial Batterers are narcissists. They might have other personality disorders in addition.

The narcissistic Serial Batterer exhibits the following behaviors:

- He shows an extreme sense of self-importance and self-worth.
- With other people, he constantly talks about himself and his interests. He has an endless and excessive need for attention and admiration from others.
- His relationship with his wife or girlfriend is not a normal loving relationship of give and take. He only takes and takes. Like an insect parasite that sucks blood from an animal or sap from a tree, the narcissist is a parasite who seems to suck what he needs emotionally and physically from a woman. He has no regard for her needs. He values her only in relation to how she can meet his continual needs.

- He feels no responsibility whatsoever to give anything back to her, even though she continually neglects her own needs and the needs of her children in trying to satisfy *his* needs. He feels entitled to this care.
- When his needs are not satisfied in the manner he believes he's entitled to, he erupts in violence.

This man has what is known as a love-hate relationship with himself. On the outside he may seem self-confident and well-pleased with his achievements and enthusiastic about his plans for future achievements. On the inside, his self-esteem is very easily bruised, and he is overly sensitive to what other people say. As a result, he often responds aggressively to the slightest criticism, even when it's presented in a constructive and non-threatening manner.

In his family relationships, he is emotionally shallow.

This means he's unable to feel sorry for his wife or girlfriend if she is in emotional distress or physical pain.

Although he sometimes appears to show concern for his partner and children, usually he is only trying to manipulate them to get what he wants from them. Once he gets it, he quickly changes back into the demanding parasite.

The self-centered behavior of the narcissistic batterer is like that of an infant or very young child.

It's normal for an infant to make huge emotional and physical demands on its mother, ignoring her need for sleep or anything else. Whenever her baby demands feeding, changing, or cuddling, she gives it.

Of course, no one expects an infant to give back to its mother the same care or concern. Nor is the baby trying to make its mother feel tired or stressed on purpose. The mother's caring and concern are based on love *from* the mother *to* the child. She knows the baby doesn't love her yet; instead, the baby *needs* her.

As an infant grows into a child of five or six, he or she learns that relationships between people are more than one-way self-centered demands. Children begin to see that biting or throwing a tantrum is not the way to get what they want from others, and that excessive demands and selfishness don't build satisfying relationships with others. So these "infantile" behaviors begin to disappear and are replaced with personality characteristics that are more socially acceptable.

A normal child eventually becomes capable of feeling that the well-being of other people is as important as his or her own well-being.

Many children, however, don't grow up according to this ideal. They may experience extreme emotional or physical neglect. If their minds and bodies can't develop normally, their feelings can't develop normally. They never grow out of their natural childhood stage of narcissism.

Emotionally, these children *stay* children and remain narcissistic and self-centered even as adults.

The Serial Batterer who is diagnosed as having a narcissistic personality disorder shows many of the same behaviors as a narcissistic child. When he doesn't get his way:

- He goes into a tantrum, like a child, but he is much more dangerous. He throws furniture and breaks windows, mirrors, and almost anything in sight.
- His tantrums include hysterical sobbing, threats, and foul language.
- Often, he orders his family and friends out of the house.

Jealousy

The way he relates to his partner is also childlike. We expect a three-year-old to be possessive or jealous, especially when the mother is showing affection to someone else. But when the Serial Batterer thinks his wife or girlfriend has given "too much" attention to another person, especially a man, he feels threatened and accuses her of having an affair, forbidding her to speak with the man again.

He is similarly intimidated by her relationships with relatives and friends—even her parents and her children.

His jealousy is beyond childlike; it's extremely abnormal.

The narcissistic batterer doesn't love his partner any more than a baby loves its mother. To him, the reason a woman exists is for his convenience. To him, she is only a caretaker who must attend to his personal desires while ignoring her own.

When she's pregnant

If his partner is pregnant, he generally sees the future child as competition. He doesn't want anything to interfere with the woman's attention and ability to "feed" his own needs. He is so afraid of taking second place to the newborn, he not only beats his pregnant partner but also makes obvious attempts to kill the fetus.

One victim testified that she suffered a miscarriage after her husband beat her in the stomach with a large pipe.

Another described how her husband struck her in the face with a baseball bat, knocking her down a steep staircase. As she tried to get up, he began to stomp on her chest.

One woman described how her husband pulled her out of bed and kicked her in the stomach with hard leather boots, mumbling that he was sick of hearing about the babies. She was six months pregnant with twins. When she wouldn't give him her last ten dollars because she needed it for prenatal vitamins, he went berserk, forcing her to swallow a bottle of rubbing alcohol. In minutes she began having severe cramps and pleaded with him to drive her to the hospital. He dropped her off at the emergency entrance and drove off.

"I lost both my babies that night," she said. "He showed no guilt for what he'd done. I hate him. He's a monster. An absolute monster."

The batterer's ability to end his partner's pregnancy gives him great control—a way to inflict terrible emotional and physical pain on his victim.

The pain from her physical wounds might go away sooner than her grief about losing a child she wanted.

Biting

One of the most primitive and animal-like behaviors of the narcissistic batterer is biting. Far more powerful than when he was a child, this adult abuser uses his teeth to tear flesh from his victim's arms, legs, and body, causing serious injury and permanent scarring.

People who interview victims of battering are amazed to see just how often this occurs. And the victim always seems surprised when asked if her husband or boyfriend bites her. She can't imagine that anyone else would know such behavior was even a possibility. But the interviewer sees it all too often.

The man who bites his victim is perhaps one of the more disturbed and dangerous of the Serial Batterers.

The Antisocial Batterer

One man attacked his wife and pounded her with both fists in the middle of a crowded courtroom.

Another threatened his wife with a loaded gun inside a church. The choir stopped singing and watched in disbelief.

Among Serial Batterers, the antisocial batterer is the most shamelessly aggressive.

While some abusers are careful to batter their mates only in private, this batterer beats his wife or girlfriend in restaurants, nightclubs, and at parties in front of strangers, friends, family, and neighbors. He:

- batters his wife or girlfriend in public
- can't control his impulses

- doesn't care about the consequences of his behavior
- is constantly in trouble with the law
- batters other people besides his partner, including his children.

Because he has no control over his impulses and doesn't care about the consequences of his behavior, the antisocial batterer is the most likely to come to the attention of police. His extensive criminal record often includes theft, drug abuse, and numerous acts of personal violence. He gets into violent fights with everyone—neighbors, co-workers, employers. Battering his partner is only a sideline.

Heartless indifference

He has not the slightest interest in the rights of anyone else and disregards the most basic needs of his children.

Even when his family needs food and medicine, or the rent and utilities are past due, he blows his paycheck on gambling, alcohol, or drugs, then demands the savings of his partner. If his demands are refused, he threatens her and the children until she gives in. He is very aware that he can intimidate and manipulate her by abusing the children.

He does not hesitate to use a knife, stick, or belt on his own children or to hold a gun to their heads.

The antisocial abuser is a frequent job hopper who has long periods of unemployment, either quitting or getting fired because of his antisocial behavior.

Paul griped that his boss had it in for him, firing him for unsatisfactory work that he was ordered to do even though he hadn't been trained to do it. What Paul didn't mention was that his supervisors and co-workers had to physically hold him after he attacked another employee with a knife.

The antisocial batterer takes no responsibility for his job losses, claiming he's been wrongly victimized. Yet he tends to get into the same kind of trouble from one job to another.

As a result, he is constantly dependent on others for money and support and feels entitled to have his wife, parents, friends, and even his children come to his aid. After gobbling up their money and emotions until they have nothing left to give, he moves on to new relationships. But he never quite ends an old relationship, particularly with his wife, in case he can still squeeze something from her.

As we would expect of anyone who spends his life lying, stealing, conning, manipulating, and using others, the antisocial Serial Batterer has great difficulty keeping any close personal relationships.

The Borderline Batterer

"Bob couldn't handle being alone," recalled his widow. "Whenever I left the house to go to the store he was like a crazy man. He insisted on knowing where I was going and how long I'd be gone. On many occasions he would follow me. He attached himself to me like a fetus. One night he got very depressed and threatened to kill me and then himself. When he went to the back of the house, I grabbed my two kids, ran out the door, jumped in the car, and drove away.

I spent the next three nights at a local shelter. He looked for me, but on the third night he shot himself in the head with his gun. I guess I'll never know how painful it must have been for him to feel so alone. But he caused it to be that way."

Bob is an example of a batterer with a borderline personality disorder.
- He is extremely unsure of his own identity and often feels "alienated" or detached from other people.
- He has mood swings.
- He often abuses alcohol and drugs.
- He is very dependent on his wife or girlfriend for his emotional needs.

- He fears being abandoned.
- He often threatens suicide, and he might commit murder and then suicide.

Identity problems

The Serial Batterer with a borderline personality disorder suffers from what is known as a severe *identity disturbance.* That is, he's always questioning who he is, what he is, and why he is. He may consider himself a Republican on Monday, a Democrat on Tuesday, and neither one by the end of the week. Likewise, he may believe in individual choice on abortion one month but cross the street and take up with the anti-abortion picketers the next.

His beliefs change frequently, and he finds himself hunting for an identity or sense of self that he never seems to find.

As a result, he often has intense periods of *alienation*—moments when he feels totally detached and isolated from everyone in the world. These feelings are especially intense when he is separated from his wife or girlfriend. His emotional distress can become so overwhelming that he loses any sense of purpose or interest in life. He sees suicide as a way out.

Although the *threat* of suicide is a common technique used by many Category 3 abusers to manipulate others into giving in to their demands, most don't follow through. Their threats usually stop once they get what they want.

But the abuser who is likely to commit murder-suicide is the Serial Batterer with a borderline personality disorder.

Mood swings

Many victims of this type of batterer say they can sense when he's about to explode. He begins to appear withdrawn, anxious, and irritable.

He argues and complains about many little things. His mood swings do not go from a state of intense energy to deep depression—which is known as *manic-depressive behavior.* Instead, he swings from a more or less normal emotional state to one in which he feels extreme anxiety, rejection, and fear of being alone.

Like the relationships of other Serial Batterers with personality disorders, this abuser's relationships with other people are filled with problems. Although he can deal fairly normally with people for a short time, his mood swings create hostility and arguments, making it impossible for him to keep up a steady relationship over a period of time. He might have been separated and divorced many times. Of course, he blames others for such problems.

Extreme dependency

Although he tries to look as if he's in control of the relationship with his wife or girlfriend, he's actually extremely dependent on her for his emotional needs.

If she tries to end the relationship, he uses different tactics to keep her within his control and will do anything to prevent his being left alone.

"Anything" includes promising to get help for his problems. But like all Serial Batterers, he will *not* follow through once he has his partner back where he wants her. He finds fault with his therapist after one or two sessions, or uses some other excuse to drop out.

Threatens suicide

His most typical tactic is threatening to kill himself if she leaves. He holds loaded guns to his head, slashes his wrists, or overdoses on prescription drugs. If he succeeds in making his victim feel responsible or guilty enough to stay in the relationship, the cycle simply repeats itself.

If he doesn't succeed in controlling her with threats of harming himself, he beats her more severely and threatens to harm her and her children—with guns, knives, bricks, gasoline, or fire. If she does leave him, he follows, stalking and abusing her until she returns. Because she is one of the few anchors he has for his own identity, her going away leaves him without a focus.

Feels isolated

When jailed, his most painful experience is not so much the loss of freedom but the loss of control over his partner. Without the chance to attach himself to another woman, his sense of isolation, alienation, and dependency overwhelms him.

He's a binge drinker who uses alcohol and drugs to escape his feelings of emptiness and lack of interest or purpose. But substance abuse also adds fuel to his aggressive fire, taking away his inhibitions and allowing his aggression to flow freely. Alcohol and drugs give him what he sees as a good excuse for his violence.

The Histrionic Batterer

"It's over, buddy," said the judge, issuing a restraining order that prohibited Ron from contacting or seeing his estranged wife. "If you continue to pursue her, you know what the consequences are."

Ron acted as if he'd been given the death penalty. As he turned to walk out of the courtroom, his body began to tremble and his lips quivered. Claiming he could not go on without his wife, he began to cry hysterically. When his elderly mother opened the door for him, he appeared to faint and fell to the floor—after making certain his fall would be cushioned by outstretched arms. As his mother cradled him in her arms, telling him everything would be all right, his sister ran to help him, and the rest of the family began screaming for help.

Even his wife, the victim, ran to get the help of two police officers. When the officers rushed to assist him, Ron cried and waved them away. Placing his arms around the shoulders of his mother and sister, he got up from the courtroom floor and slowly went down the stairs, murmuring that he would kill himself and get out of everybody's life.

"No one cares anyway," he cried. "No one."

This is the Serial Batterer who has the personality disorder known as histrionic.

The word *histrionic* (pronounced hiss-tri-ON-ik) means overacting and theatrical. Like an actor, the histrionic batterer exaggerates his emotions to fool his audience.

- He uses hysterical behaviors, emotions, and violent outbursts to control his partner and others.
- He threatens suicide to manipulate others.
- He may seem friendly and charming on the outside, but he is cold and insecure on the inside.
- He gets away with violent and criminal behavior by convincing others he has no control over his feelings.
- He has a huge craving for excitement, feeling his life is boring. Violence is another dramatic event to liven up his existence—as are promiscuous sex, uncontrolled gambling, and alcohol and drug abuse.

He is an actor who plays his moods and emotions in overly dramatic ways. He responds to normal events with nothing less than Oscar-winning performances.

The slightest rejection, failure, or disappointment causes him to plead for reassurance and comfort.

If he thinks his wife or girlfriend is going to leave him, he stages childish tantrums in front of family members to draw them into playing a supporting role. He throws, breaks, and destroys anything he can: windows, mirrors, furniture, doors, car windshields. Following his outbursts he might curl up on the floor like a child, begging his family and friends to rescue him from his made-up misery and pain.

He knows that if he can convince them he has no control over his condition, they will give him the attention and care he desires. He wants to be seen as a helpless man who is not responsible for his behavior, and who desperately needs others to rescue him from what he sees as his unfair life.

The histrionic batterer pretends HE is the victim.

If the police are called to his home to break up a fight, he cries uncontrollably and presents himself as a troubled person who desperately needs help. He has the strange ability to make people focus on him instead of his victim. As his wife slumps in the corner with a broken jaw and split lip, the family and police turn their attention to the batterer.

Attempts suicide

If he can't get the control he wants through his usual act, he increases the drama by threatening to jump from a bridge, overdose on pills, or shoot himself with a handgun. He might make shallow cuts on his wrists or mutilate himself in some other way.

I'm not suggesting that threats of suicide are always playacting. But looked at as part of an overall pattern of overly dramatic behavior, such threats are the most effective tool the histrionic batterer has to get what he wants from others.

If his tantrums and threats of suicide don't work, he becomes more aggressive, threatening his family, friends, and strangers with acts of harm and violence. If that fails, his behavior often progresses to physical attacks.

Reactions of others

Unfortunately, others too often go along with his script. Instead of ignoring him and allowing him to suffer the natural consequences of his bad behavior, they respond with great concern, feeding his already well-developed personality disorder. Although they mean well, those who respond by giving in to his demands only ensure that the same behavior will continue.

Feeding a personality disorder only makes it worse.

Giving in to the histrionic batterer gives him the two results he wants most.

- First, like the narcissist, he is able to feed his endless need for constant attention.
- Second, he gets control over his partner—the only control this intensely inadequate and extremely insecure man feels he has in the world.

He also reads more into a relationship than may exist. He makes a woman feel "crowded." If she tries to withdraw, he stalks her, attaching himself to her like a fungus.

It is during her retreat that his overly dramatic dependency on her is most obvious.

It is during her retreat that she is in the most danger.

This man is acting nearly all the time, appearing charming, overly friendly, even flirtatious in an effort to attract and please others. He performs favors with the expectation that others "owe" him, but if someone doesn't repay what he sees as a "debt," he becomes hostile, arrogant, and violent.

Friends become worthless to him if he discovers they cannot be exploited.

His only purpose in making friends is to see what he can get from them.

The Paranoid Batterer

It was Dennis's sixth criminal offense for beating his wife, and he was in court for screening and a pretrial hearing. Suspicious of everyone and everything, he began accusing the parole officer of being sexually interested in his wife, totally ignoring the parole officer's role as her legal advocate.

He had difficulty believing someone would be interested in his wife without sex being involved.

When assured of the court's interest in cases of domestic violence, Dennis remained unimpressed.

As he continued to challenge the officer's "true intentions," Dennis's wife explained that she'd tried many times to get others to help her, but her husband had always responded with jealous rage.

This is the paranoid batterer.

- He is intensely jealous.
- He is obsessed with the idea of his partner's being unfaithful to him.
- He is suspicious of everyone and usually trusts no one.
- He is cold and emotionally shallow.

An endless stream of women appear in court every day, each one reporting abuse by a husband who insists she is having an affair. Each woman describes a man who watches her every move, questions her in detail about where she was each moment of the day, and tries to force her to admit she's been unfaithful. He threatens to kill both her and her "secret" lover when he finds out who it is.

The Serial Batterer who has a paranoid personality disorder is *obsessed* with the issue of unfaithfulness.

His partner reports that she's afraid to even speak to another man for fear her partner may become violent.

His actions are almost a ritual:

- He questions family and friends about his wife.
- He follows her and listens in on her phone calls.
- He aggressively confronts her.
- He demands a confession even though he doesn't have a shred of evidence.

If family or friends try to calm his suspicions, he accuses them of being in a plot with his faithless partner.

Even when his partner has absolute proof that his suspicions are wrong, he ignores the facts and keeps searching for "hidden" evidence.

Always having to prove to himself that his first suspicions were true, he goes into a violent fit, beating and battering his victim until she's bruised and broken. Sometimes she's dead.

Commits premeditated murder

When the media report that a man killed his wife or girl-friend because he believed she was having an affair, they call it a "crime of passion." Judges and juries are often influenced by this "crime of passion" defense.

"After all," one lawyer said in defending a wife-killer, "we can all understand how a man can lose his cool over an issue of infidelity."

If murder is made *understandable*, it is closer to being made *excusable*. But murder is not excusable.

Criminal law says that if a murder is found to have been committed in a *spontaneous manner*—that is, without premeditation—the charge is often reduced to manslaughter.

Although the term "crime of passion" suggests that the murder was committed in a spontaneous manner, many such murders are committed by men who've been stalking their partners for some time.

In fact, the murderer had been thinking about stalking his victim and had planned his actions well ahead of time.

These murders are not committed by normal men who suddenly "lose their cool" and explode with uncontrolled passion.

Murders are often committed by men who have paranoid personality disorders and other disorders as well.

Such men are capable of the most hideous, unthinkable crimes imaginable. All in the name of passion. And love.

Suspicious of everyone

The suspicious nature of the paranoid Serial Batterer is not limited to his partner. He is intensely watchful all the time, always looking for hidden meanings in everything anyone does.

- If his boss orders a job study because costs are too high, he thinks the study is focused mainly on him, and he feels intimidated and threatened.

- When he passes a group of co-workers, he feels they are talking about him and his poor work.
- When his relatives get together, he carefully watches their conversation for signs of their encouraging his partner to leave him.

He sees hidden meaning in almost everything. To him, the world is a hostile place. He stays somewhat withdrawn from other people because he feels that others are trying to take advantage of him—and even conspiring against him. He generally trusts no one.

Even when he seems to trust some people, he is tense, always on guard, and alert for clues of their "true intentions."

Often, he misreads the intentions of others, but when confronted with the truth, he immediately tries to clear himself of blame for his opinions. When confronted about beating his partner, he denies it or excuses his behavior by blaming everything and everyone but himself.

He justifies his aggression by claiming he was provoked by something that someone else was responsible for.

As a cold and emotionally shallow person, he has difficulty expressing any warm and gentle feelings, and he lacks the ability to love.

Even though his extreme jealousy makes it seem that he cares for his victim, he is actually a predator who stalks and beats his partner with a total absence of self-blame, remorse, or concern.

The Obsessive-Compulsive Batterer

At his son's Little League games, Frank challenged every call of the umpire's. When his son hit the ball but got called out before making it to base, Frank stood up and screamed at the child for not running fast enough. When the boy missed a swing, he loudly scolded him for holding the bat wrong.

Once when his son allowed a run to score, Frank screamed, stomped out of the ball park, and drove off. Two games later, he physically threatened the coach and was permanently ejected from the park.

Frank has an obsessive-compulsive personality disorder. He is also a Serial Batterer.

- He has an intense need to control his surroundings.
- He is obsessed with rules and order.
- He is a perfectionist about his own performance and other people's.
- He is obsessed with small, unimportant details.
- Leisure is an extension of the workplace.
- He often gets away with his crimes of battering because he tends to hold a position of respect.

A woman involved with an obsessive-compulsive partner often describes their personal relationship as if she were a military recruit under the command of a drill sergeant. In his interactions with others he is controlling, demanding, overbearing, formal, and critical. His relationship with his family is a dictatorship. Everything is his way and his way alone. No compromise, no negotiation. When his partner tries to question or challenge him, he beats her.

He doesn't have a partner, he has a terrorized victim.

He tells her when to eat and when to sleep; what to cook and what not to cook; when to wake up and when to clean house. He tells her whether she can go to work or stay home. Even their sex life is formalized and scheduled.

Janet's husband set aside one hour every second week on the same night to have sex with her. Any attempt to interest him in sex before their scheduled time was useless. When they did have sexual relations, it was mechanical and totally lacking in any closeness.

She avoided the words "making love,'" explaining that their sex had nothing to do with love: "Like everything else, it was simply something on his list of things to do."

Some obsessive-compulsive batterers do feel a desire to express their innermost feelings at times. But when they try, say many, they become stiff and emotionally blocked.

Another woman told of her husband's inability to express warm emotion. "When others would cry, his eyes would always remain clear and dry. When others would hug, he always stood at a distance. When others would tell him, 'I love you,' he would respond, 'Me, too.'"

Needs structure

The Serial Batterer with an obsessive-compulsive personality disorder is extremely insecure.

Keeping his life structured and orderly makes him feel in control—at least for a little while. He constantly makes "to do" lists, and when he finishes 15 of the 20 items on his list, he feels good. He has a sense of order and control over his life. But his obsession with unimportant details almost always means he never finishes his more important goals.

His deep fear of failure and rejection makes him anxious and uncertain about trying to accomplish more important things.

If he can waste his time on simple details, he doesn't have to take the real risks of attacking anything more difficult.

He can say he did his best and blame any failures on not having enough time. His obsession with unimportant details is actually the attempt of a very insecure man to avoid the pain of possible failure.

His co-workers usually don't see the down side. To them, he is the "human machine." They see his compulsive work habits as those of someone who is organized, efficient, reliable, and effective. After all, by spending ten hours a day working on unimportant things, he always *looks* busy, *feels* busy, and *is* busy.

When he fails to complete his more important tasks, he simply justifies it by saying that he had too much to do. In reality, his focus on unimportant tasks makes him an extremely inefficient and nonproductive worker.

His "perfectionism" is a desperate try at avoiding shame and failure. Ironically, he ends up feeling guilty, worthless, and frustrated anyway, because he fails to put the items on his "to do" list in the order of their importance.

His negative feelings smolder within a volcano of mental unrest and confusion.

He transforms his unrest into unrestrained violence, and he dangerously abuses his partner.

The strict obsessions of this batterer take priority over his normal work schedule. Though he may have a lot of vacation time saved up, he seldom uses it. He often postpones or cancels his vacation and gives the appearance of doing so "for the good of the company." He claims he can't afford to take time off. But below the surface, he's afraid that if he's away from work:

- he will lose control
- his temporary replacement can't be trusted
- others could discover his faults and weaknesses.

When he does take time off, his strictness with rules and performance takes away any pleasure for him and for others. He can't tell the difference between play time, leisure time, and work. To the obsessive-compulsive person, play time is simply one more way he can prove himself to others. Winning is everything; losing challenges his ego and self-image.

When his self-esteem suffers, he responds with rage and aggression.

Shirley was married to a Serial Batterer with an obsessive-compulsive personality disorder. "Living with him was like living on a military base. He treated me as if I was a new recruit," she reports.

"He not only gave me orders but also followed up each day to see if they had been carried out. If I didn't

*obey immediately, he beat me. He and his needs were
always first.*

*"Many of the things he dictated that I do were repeti-
tious and ridiculous, like polishing the silverware every
two weeks. One morning when he told me to polish the
silverware I had a sick child to care for and two others
who needed help with homework. That evening when
he learned that I did not do as I had been told, he went
crazy. After punching me in the face and chest, he held
me down and handcuffed me to the bedpost.*

*"As I kicked and fought back, he began to bite me on
the arms and legs. Realizing what he was capable of
doing to me, I became nonverbal and passive. Finally,
he uncuffed me and ordered me to clean the silverware
as originally told. I was bleeding from the forehead and
asked if I could attend to it. He said only when I finished with the silverware."*

Escapes detection

Often, this kind of batterer becomes highly educated. It's
not that he's more intelligent than other Serial Batterers;
it's that his life—unlike the chaos-filled lives of antisocial,
narcissistic, or histrionic batterers—is organized and strictly
focused, and he knows how to follow rules.

He tends to seek a career in the military, law, law enforcement, or politics, and a diploma gives him access to
high-status jobs of power and control.

**He uses his professional status to avoid detection and
responsibility for the abuse of his wife.**

If his abuse is exposed, his position helps shield him from
the punishments that less powerful men receive for the
same violent behavior.

I don't mean to suggest that most batterers who are obsessive-compulsive reach such positions. Many find themselves unemployed or filling low-status jobs. What I do
want to emphasize is that the batterer who has an obses-

sive-compulsive personality disorder is the most likely of the Serial Batterers to go into professions in which his power helps shield him from the consequences of beating his wife.

His ability to get and keep positions of power and control is dangerous.

- How many police officers would arrest a fellow officer for abusing his wife?
- How many prosecutors would prosecute another attorney?
- How many judges would jail a fellow judge?

In addition, men who appear professional are simply more believable than men who do not. The way this Serial Batterer dresses, the car he drives, the neighborhood he lives in—even the way he carries himself—all are *symbols* that give unspoken messages to those around him.

It's his clever use of these symbols that helps him avoid responsibility for his behavior.

A movie on TV dramatized the true story of a woman who had appeared in a court many times to plead for protection from a husband she described as dangerously brutal. Despite the evidence of physical abuse, the batterer was always released, with almost no action taken, because he presented himself in a dignified, well-spoken, and professional manner. Finally, after a beating in which the abuse was too severe to ignore, the judge ordered the batterer held in a local hospital for a psychiatric evaluation.

The man's professional appearance and ability to speak well made it hard for the hospital psychiatrist to ignore the "symbols" and concentrate on the facts, especially when the conversation revealed that both men shared similar hobbies and interests. Based on that brief interview, the psychiatrist saw no reason to deny the defendant a pass to leave the hospital temporarily. The man immediately went to his wife's house and murdered her, stabbing her 30 to 40 times with a large knife.

To the average person, violence to a spouse, or to any woman, is impossible to understand. Judges, prosecutors, and other court employees also have difficulty understanding the depth and scale of what they hear each day.

Victims tell how they are knocked down stairs in late pregnancy and how jagged objects are rammed up their vaginas. They testify how loaded guns are held to their heads and to the heads of their children. They describe how lips, nipples, and fingernails are ripped from their bodies by their abusers.

Crime photographs of the lifeless bodies of women and children are seen far too often. Still, it is difficult for law enforcement personnel to fully understand what they see and hear.

Such abuse is even harder to believe when the batterer not only looks like a judge or lawyer, but also sounds and acts like one.

Combinations of personality disorders

Many Serial Batterers don't fit neatly into one of the six personality disorders. Many of them exhibit behaviors typical of two or more of these disorders.

For example, a Serial Batterer could be diagnosed as being a borderline, narcissistic, and antisocial batterer all at the same time.

Such men are exceptionally dangerous and deadly.

Summary

- Psychiatrists have identified many kinds of personality disorders, each one characterized by a particular set of behaviors.
- Among Category 3 or Serial Batterers, six kinds of personality disorders show up over and over. These are:

1. Narcissistic Personality Disorder
2. Antisocial Personality Disorder
3. Borderline Personality Disorder
4. Histrionic Personality Disorder
5. Paranoid Personality Disorder
6. Obsessive-Compulsive Personality Disorder.

- Some Serial Batterers show different combinations of different personality disorders.
- All Serial Batterers are extremely dangerous.

Chapter 5

Category 2:
The Sporadic Batterer

"Don't get me wrong. He doesn't hit me all the time,"
said the badly bruised woman who sat facing the pro-
bation officer. "We've been married ten years, and I guess
he beat me about four times. On two of those occa-
sions, however, he could easily have killed me.

"He once held me on the floor and rammed the tip of
a loaded revolver between my legs. He accused me of
having an affair with his best friend. When I tried to
convince him it wasn't true, he removed the gun and
struck me across the face with it, breaking my jaw. Then
he curled up in the corner of the room and cried like a
baby."

Recognizing the type

Most women who are battered are in relationships with
men who fall into the large middle area on the Batterer's
Continuum. These men are Category 2 or Sporadic Batterers. *Sporadic* means happening from time to time.

BATTERER'S CONTINUUM

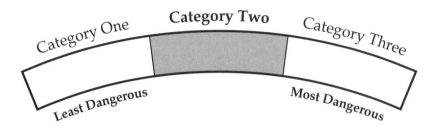

To understand this very large, broad category of abuser, we have to know what kind of men make up the other two categories at the extreme ends of the Batterer's Continuum: the Category 1 or Remorseful Batterer and the Category 3 or Serial Batterer.

Without describing these two extremes, it's very difficult to explain this in-between batterer. His violent attacks are not ongoing, like the Serial Batterer's. Neither are his attacks rare events, like the Remorseful Batterer's.

Nevertheless, the Sporadic Batterer is a very dangerous man. Think of him as being a *mixture* of the two extremes on the Batterer's Continuum.

This batterer's history

- He could have a history of abusing women.
- His emotions and aggression are easily triggered by outside events, but come primarily from the rage that exists entirely within himself.
- Although his character defects are not numerous enough to be diagnosed as a full-blown personality disorder, these character defects are serious.
- His violence occurs irregularly. The same man can go several months without committing an assault, but at times the calm between beatings lasts only a few days.
- While he may not be as *habitually violent* as the Serial Batterer, he will almost certainly continue to batter unless he is forced to stop.

- Because he beats his victim less frequently and perhaps less brutally than a Serial Batterer does, he is somewhat less dangerous.

But his victim is always at risk of being seriously injured or killed during any one of his rampages.

Proceed with caution

The Sporadic Batterer is better able to function in society than the Serial Batterer because he has fewer character defects. He doesn't have enough of these defects to be labeled as actually having a particular personality disorder.

But he still has too many bad qualities to be considered a Category 1 batterer.

Perhaps we can best describe him as a *different version* of the Category 3 abuser.

Yet the Sporadic Batterer is not merely a milder version of the Serial Batterer.

What triggers his violence is different.

- The violent episodes of the Remorseful Batterer are brought on mainly by outside trauma.
- The ongoing violence of the Serial Batterer comes from his own deep-seated personality disorder and internal conflicts.

Violence committed by the Sporadic Batterer is triggered by the stress of circumstances in his life *and* by conflicts inside himself.

Comparison with other batterers

The Sporadic Batterer has some limited ability to control his impulses. As a result, he does not always cause serious injury to his victim or use weapons to make his assaults more harmful. Compared with a Serial Batterer, he is less likely to kill his partner, though he is certainly capable of doing so. If he stalks his victim, terrorizes her or her children, or commits any of the other horrible acts of violence so typical of the Serial Batterer, he does so with somewhat less intensity and frequency.

The Sporadic Batterer who beats his wife is less likely to have beaten her before marriage, and he's had fewer violent relationships with other women in his life. He is less likely to have a criminal record for domestic violence or petty crime. If he is arrested, he responds better to orders to stay away from his partner.

One way to see the difference in behavior between the Category 2 and the Category 3 batterer is to measure the *level of violence* that takes place in an attack, and the *frequency* of the attacks.

Use of alcohol and drugs

When it comes to alcohol and drugs, there is very little difference between the Sporadic Batterer and the Serial Batterer. Both use drinking and drugs for the same reasons:

- to hide the insecurities that come from their many personality defects
- to find a temporary escape from what they dislike about themselves
- to enjoy a false sense of confidence
- to have an excuse for their aggressive behavior.

Both kinds of batterers totally deny responsibility for their brutal violence, and they blame the alcohol or drugs. They frequently get roaring drunk, ruthlessly beat their partners, and blame everything on the pretense of having been drinking and losing control.

It's when *any* batterer has been using alcohol or drugs that he is most explosive, unpredictable, and dangerous.

Both types of abusers have strong feelings of insecurity and inadequacy, which lie just below the surface of their everyday behavior. When these men drink, their insecurities seem to ooze from their emotional pores like sweat and are easily transformed into violent rages.

When batterers drink, it's hard for anyone to tell the Sporadic Batterer from the Serial Batterer.

In one other situation they also behave very much alike: when separated from their partners. When the batterer lacks his wife or girlfriend to prove that he has power and control, his insecurities become too much for him to bear, and he goes on a rampage. Here, too, he is able to blame his behavior on an outside cause: the woman who left him.

> To leave a batterer safely, especially when children are involved, a woman must have a safety plan and a support system. These are described in Chapter 12.

Can this man be rehabilitated?

If there's a Sporadic Batterer in your life, always view him as a serious threat to your safety. This doesn't mean he is a hopeless case. You don't have to write him off as being incapable of change, though I must tell you there's not much evidence that the treatment of this batterer is successful.

Many therapists believe that the outlook for his rehabilitation is very gloomy.

In some instances, however, he might respond to treatment and learn more acceptable behaviors. That's because:

- He has some degree of remorse, insight, and motivation—all of which are necessary for him to change.
- He has some ability to bond with his wife or girlfriend and children.
- He is less disturbed than the Serial Batterer.

The fact that he is not as vicious or as disturbed as the Serial Batterer means that the chances of his being able to change in the future are not as bad. I am *not* saying that his chances of being able to change are good. But given the right circumstances, it's *possible* he may change.

Because his motivation to change is limited, it's necessary to increase his motivation.

This is best accomplished through:
- his partner's separating from him
- the judge's putting him in jail.

Both of these methods are described in Chapters 10 and 11.

In the end, it's the victim of this man's abuse who must decide what to do about the rest of her life.

Whatever that decision is, I urge her to make it only after:

- reviewing the behaviors typical of each category of batterer
- using the Batterer's Continuum to help her decide what category her abuser falls into
- facing her individual circumstances without illusion and false hope.

A victim of a Sporadic Batterer must proceed with extreme caution.

Summary

- Most men who batter women fall into the large middle position on the Batterer's Continuum.
- The emotions and aggressions of the Category 2 or Sporadic Batterer are easily triggered by outside events, but they often come from the rage that exists entirely within himself.
- Although his character defects are not numerous enough to be diagnosed as creating a full-blown personality disorder, he does have some serious character defects.
- The Sporadic Batterer is somewhat less dangerous than the Serial Batterer, but he will almost certainly continue to batter unless he is forced to stop.
- When it comes to alcohol and drugs, there is very little difference between the Sporadic Batterer and the Serial Batterer.

- Although most Sporadic Batterers are not good candidates for treatment, some may be sincerely motivated to change and should not be written off entirely.
- The victim of a Sporadic Batterer is always at risk of being seriously injured or even killed during any one of his rampages. She needs a safety plan for herself and her children, whether she decides to stay with him, or leave him temporarily while he sticks with treatment, or leave him permanently.

Chapter 6

What Batterers Have in Common

Her lips quivered and her hands trembled as she graphically told what her batterer had done to her.

As she described the many occasions on which he'd vandalized her property, sent her threatening letters, kicked in her door, and held a loaded 9 mm gun to her right temple, I felt certain we'd talked before. I found myself filling in details she'd omitted—accurately, as it turned out—as if I knew what she was going to say before she said it. However, we'd never met before.

Over the 20 years I've been dealing with abusers and the women they victimize, I've heard the same stories of abuse reported over and over by different women.

The behaviors they describe are so similar that their stories echo in my mind.

In case after case, the woman testifies how her husband or boyfriend:
- broke her windshield
- slashed the tires on her car
- entered her home through the bedroom window
- beat her
- destroyed her furniture
- left through the front door.

In addition, the women who are targeted by such men report telephone harassment, use of weapons, threats of murder-suicide, biting, childlike tantrums, and stalking. These behaviors are reported so often that an experienced prosecutor is often able to predict which behaviors a victim is likely to describe.

In case after case, it's alarming to hear testimony that reveals:

- how ruthless these batterers can be
- how similar their behaviors are.

Nearly all Serial Batterers, and many Sporadic Batterers, have certain behaviors in common.

In this chapter we look at the characteristics and behaviors that the great majority of batterers have in common with each other. *Not included in this discussion of batterers is the man who fits the profile of the true Remorseful Batterer.*

How dangerous a batterer's behaviors are depends on where the individual stands on the Batterer's Continuum.

The farther he is to the right on the continuum, the more likely his actions will continue.

And because certain behavior patterns are so similar from one batterer to another, we can pretty accurately predict *how* his actions will continue.

A number of these patterns are part of the six personality disorders that many Serial Batterers exhibit. But it's important to look at some of these characteristics again, because:

- stopping abuse starts with knowing what kind of personality disorders the batterer has
- pinning down where one type of personality disorder ends and another begins can be difficult.

When a woman or her family and friends recognize that her partner has many characteristics of the Sporadic or the Serial Batterer, it is absolutely necessary to understand the enormous risks she faces.

Ignoring these warning signs is extremely dangerous.

Any woman who plans to continue a relationship with this kind of man needs to study these characteristics very carefully.

The signs of a personality disorder usually show up early in a relationship. In many cases they show up on the first date.

If you know what they are, these signs can act as red flags, as warning signals.

They alert a woman to the dangers that may lurk deep in the shadows of the relationship.

• *Never* expect this batterer to change his behavior.

• *Never* think things will improve after marriage.

The possibility that a Serial Batterer will change is almost nonexistent.

Psychological-emotional similarities

Denies and minimizes

Most batterers are experts at denying responsibility for their behavior. They are so expert at denial that they convince themselves—and even others—that they are not responsible for the injuries of their victims.

Batterers with long criminal records for beating their partners often deny all responsibility for their behavior.

It's amazing how anyone can be arrested several times for savagely beating his wife and repeatedly deny personal blame for his actions. But these batterers do.

Peter had been booked six times in four months for attacking his wife. He claimed she overreacted during arguments. When it was pointed out to him that each time she appeared in court she had cuts, scrapes, and bruises to her face and body, he answered by saying that she was clumsy and often fell.

Martin had more than 12 domestic violence arrests in 12 months. He claimed that his neighbors were always

*calling the police and reporting a disturbance just to get
even with him over something else. When it was pointed
out that his wife was taken to a hospital emergency room
after the last incident, he claimed she was injured by
one of the neighbors during a scuffle.*

Obviously much of this denial is an attempt of the
batterer's to avoid the *consequences* of his violence. But it's
amazing how capable these batterers are of blaming others, including their victims, for the injuries that result.

How can a man shatter his wife's face and body with his
fist, threaten her with a loaded gun, and then deny any
responsibility for it?

**Batterers have the tendency to downplay the obvious or
even to deny the attack altogether.**

Though his victim's injuries may be severe or disabling,
the batterer reduces the attack to a minor event. He even
reduces the size of the weapon he used.

*After one batterer was shown that his wife had suf-
fered a serious spinal injury and a broken shoulder in
an assault, he insisted he'd hit her only once. "She
slipped and fell over a coffee table," he said. When challenged by prosecutors with evidence that he'd also held
a knife to her throat, he said it was only a small pocket-
knife.*

*Another defendant beat his victim unconscious with
a metal pipe but insisted he'd struck her only twice.
More than 15 large pipe-shaped bruises covered her
arms, legs, and back.*

*One batterer, after being arrested for pulling and fir-
ing a loaded gun into the bed where his wife slept,
claimed that it was just "a small broken gun" that acci-
dentally fired when he dropped it.*

**There isn't a Serial Batterer who doesn't deny or greatly
minimize the violence he's done.**

- If he's confronted with limited evidence, he firmly denies the event.
- If he's confronted with absolute evidence, he simply minimizes it.

Rationalizes and externalizes

Batterers are very clever at convincing themselves and others that they were provoked by their partners or by conditions beyond their control. They blame their violent rages on money problems, or their children's misbehavior, or the refusal of their wives to follow their orders.

Putting blame outside oneself is known as *externalizing.* **It's closely tied to the batterer's denial of responsibility for his own violent behavior.**

When the batterer explains that he killed his wife because she was having an affair, he is not only *externalizing* (putting blame outside himself), he is also *rationalizing* or naming a *reason* to try to justify his violence.

"She made me do it by running around on me," he says. If it is proven that his wife has *not* been unfaithful, he says, "She was thinking about doing it." He adds a final justification: "Any man who would let his wife mess around on him is a fool."

Let's say his wife *is* having an affair. Her responsibility for her own actions does not give someone else a license to physically abuse or kill her—even when that someone is her husband.

There is no reason that can excuse violence.

When a murderer gives reasons such as job stress, grief, jealousy, self-defense, or any other external cause for his own violence, others sometimes support his reasons. They talk about understanding *why* he was violent. Or a defense attorney persuades listeners to weigh such reasons.

When the news media simply report the reason given by a batterer, that reason tends to become accepted as fact. Such responses from the media and others are known as *enabling* responses. They enable the batterer to continue his battering. They feed into his personality disorder.

A supportive or enabling response not only tends to justify, explain, and excuse violence but also helps the violence to continue.

Lacks remorse and empathy

It's frightening to see how little remorse many batterers show following the beating and maiming of their partners. They show absolute detachment and a chilling lack of compassion or understanding for the pain and misery suffered by their victims—which we call a lack of empathy.

Although the batterer's inability to feel remorse and empathy is as shocking as the crime itself, this inability is a common symptom of his personality disorder. It's also a common symptom of his inability to bond with other people. If he cannot bond with his partner, he cannot sense her pain.

Cannot love or bond

Research shows that most batterers were brought up in domestic "war zones." As babies and young children, they grew up in hostile surroundings where emotional and physical violence were "normal."

- Instead of feeling safe, they felt threatened.
- Instead of feeling secure, they felt distressed.
- Instead of love, they experienced rejection.
- Instead of learning trust, they learned to be fearful and watchful.

Domestic war zones are incubators for future violence. A child who is emotionally starved in early childhood stands a good chance of growing up emotionally unstable.

This might *explain* the violence. But it does not *excuse* it.

In fact, by explaining its cause we can make an even stronger case for the victim of a batterer to leave such relationships so her children *don't continue the cycle.*

Families that don't function in normal ways are known as *dysfunctional families*. Boys brought up in dysfunctional families, in which they are abused or see their mother being abused, grow up without learning how to bond with other people. If you can't trust Daddy, whom *can* you trust?

If the bonding stage of a child's life is destroyed, the child is destroyed. If the child is destroyed, his ability to bond as an adult is destroyed. He becomes a predator, a stalker, a batterer—sometimes a killer—who has no conscience.

When it comes to love, the Serial Batterer is emotionally crippled. He is incapable of respecting or responding to the needs of his mate.

Jerry, age 21, sat in his therapist's office and cried like a child. He described how he'd hit his wife with the leg of a broken chair, striking her several times as she lay on the bedroom floor bleeding severely from her forehead. She begged him to stop, but he kept beating her. After she passed out, he took her to the hospital where he learned that his 19-year-old wife, the mother of two young sons, had permanent brain damage. She would be paralyzed the rest of her life.

As Jerry continued to cry, he and the therapist discussed his feelings about the hideous act he'd committed. It soon became obvious that his tears were not tears of remorse over the pain and suffering he'd caused his wife. He was crying because he thought his wife would leave him—that he would lose possession of her. In two hours with his therapist, he showed not the slightest guilt, grief, or concern for his wife's welfare and well-being.

What some people see as the batterer's "love" is really an extremely unhealthy dependency. The batterer possesses his mate. He controls, dominates, and absorbs her. Her only usefulness to him lies in how she can feed his many needs.

This is not love.

A Serial Batterer is not capable of love.

Is emotionally intense

What is it about batterers that attracts women to them in the first place? Probably the emotional intensity they display. Though Serial Batterers—and many Sporadic Batterers—are social parasites and misfits, they are anything but dull. They usually live on society's edge. As a result, a relationship with such a man may promise to be very exciting.

When I was a small boy I greatly admired one of my uncles and looked forward to my outings with him. I jumped from bridges with him into a deep lake and rode in his car at high speeds. I walked with him across a train trestle and clung dangerously to its side as the train passed. This uncle shared his food and beer with me. He also shared his craziness. He was intense, and it was exciting to be with him. In fact, he was more like a playmate than a relative.

My uncle lived on society's edge. Though his explosions of intensity brought him periodic highs in life, it eventually brought him death. In a pre-dawn fog, his speeding car struck a large tree. It was believed he was drunk at the time.

Much later I came to realize that his behaviors reflected a personality disorder. I learned that back in the days when battered women stayed in the closet, he frequently assaulted my aunt.

Just as I was drawn to my uncle's free-wheeling style, many relatively normal and well-adjusted women find themselves drawn to batterers with personality disorders. Among the factors that create chemistry between men and women, I believe that the batterer's emotional intensity triggers a strong response—especially early in the relationship.

One badly beaten newlywed explained, "He was the most exciting man I ever met. He was so much fun— until he shot me. My friends told me he was dangerous and would hurt me, but I guess I was blinded by his stimulating qualities."

Feels inadequate and depressed

Batterers have extremely low self-esteem and feel intensely inadequate. On the surface, they may give the appearance of being self-confident and arrogant. But below the surface, these men have a terrible self-image and a serious sense of inferiority.

Some batterers have identity problems—such as the batterer with a borderline personality disorder (described in Chapter 4). They are seriously disturbed by not knowing who they are. However, other batterers who do have some idea of who they are simply *do not like what they see.*

A Serial Batterer generally dislikes himself. His low self-esteem gives rise to enormous emotional conflicts inside himself. Outside himself, conflicts such as job stress, failure, and criticism don't *cause* his violence but act as triggers in *releasing* his anger and *transferring* it into violence, particularly violence against a wife or girlfriend.

One woman described how her husband's moods would change into rage whenever he'd been personally criticized or challenged. He brooded over any criticism, even when it was constructive, becoming withdrawn and sullen.

As this depressed state grew, he would explode into violent rage, beating not only her, but the children. After one scolding from his boss, she and her kids escaped from their home moments before her husband took a gun, placed it in his mouth, and pulled the trigger.

Later, she realized that his inadequacy was so severe that death was the only way out for him. She said, "His life had to be more painful than his death. It's something he confronted every hour of each day. Now he's at peace and so are we."

Feels dependent and jealous

Many batterers are pathetically dependent on the women in their lives. Just as a young child attaches itself to its mother, these men attach themselves to their wives and girlfriends to have their emotional and physical needs met on demand.

The Serial Batterer, in particular, has never let go of his emotional umbilical cord. He's carried it over his shoulder since birth, always looking to attach it to an unsuspecting victim.

Once it's attached, the woman finds it almost impossible to cut it loose. If she does, he forcibly re-attaches it to her again and again, absorbing her fragile identity until there's nothing left for him to feed on. When that happens, he quickly drapes the cord over his shoulder and looks for another victim to exploit. On finding her, he implants this emotional umbilical cord into the belly of his new prey.

This batterer tries to make his partner completely dependent on him, and in many ways he succeeds.

As intensely dependent as she may seem, there is probably nothing more intense than the dependency the batterer has on his victim.

His dependency is deeply rooted in his personality disorder.

He is obsessed with wanting his partner physically present, and when she's away he feels unbearably isolated and uncertain. This dependency often results in acts of stalking and physical violence.

He shows extreme possessiveness and jealousy, expecting to possess his wife or girlfriend in the same way he claims ownership of his car and his home—which no one has the right to take away.

To keep control and prevent anyone from helping her escape, he tries desperately to isolate her from family, friends, and potential employers.

He needs constant reassurance that he isn't losing her to someone else. So he cross-examines her in detail, demanding to know why she didn't answer the phone when he called or who she was talking to when he got a busy signal. He questions her intensely about former boyfriends, their dating habits, and even her past sexual experiences. When she is persuaded into sharing her most intimate secrets by his promise not to get angry, he beats her in a jealous rage.

The Serial Batterer is jealous of everyone—not only other men but also parents, children, and family members.

He is especially jealous of her friendships with other women because he knows they may influence her to leave him.

If she tries to escape, he goes after her to get back his "property."

Charles was facing a jail term for stalking his ex-wife. When scolded by the judge and the prosecutor, he stubbornly replied, "This is my wife and no one, absolutely no one, has the right to keep me away from her."

While awaiting sentencing, Charles was re-arrested after kidnapping his ex-wife at gunpoint. During his arraignment on new felony charges, he again declared that she belonged to him and the court had no right to interfere. After serving two years he was released and immediately began hunting her down. He was later charged with her murder.

Extreme possessiveness on the part of a Sporadic or Serial Batterer should never be confused with the jealousy of a normal man or that of a Remorseful Batterer.

Tragically for the woman who is savagely beaten and—in many instances—murdered, she is likely to see her batterer's jealous nature as flattering evidence that he cares for her. In actuality, the extent of his possessiveness is a measure of how poisonously sick and dangerously disturbed he is.

Needs to dominate emotionally

Many batterers share a similar need to constantly dominate. They can't stand to be disagreed with, and they firmly
believe that any resistance or misbehavior should be severely punished. Their intimidating and inflexible behavior guarantees that they will stay in control.

With his wife or girlfriend, the batterer allows absolutely
no room for negotiation or compromise. He does not want
her opinion and rarely asks for it.

**When he speaks, he expects her to listen and follow his
orders.**

She learns early in the relationship that any challenge to
his authority provokes a violent physical response.

He is sexist in his belief that the man should be in charge
in an intimate relationship. Although this characteristic is
shared by the majority of men throughout the world, researchers have found that batterers are significantly more
conservative and traditional in their views than men who
do not abuse women. Any challenge to his position as rul-
ing head of the family is unacceptable interference.

**Most batterers feel that a woman's place in a relation-
ship is limited to that of a caretaker.**

To him, a woman's purpose is to cater to his emotional,
physical, and sexual needs. When he is down and out, she
is to give him money. When he is jailed for his crimes, she
is to rescue him. She is his slave, and when she fails to give
him what he demands, he beats her.

Unfortunately, this man's sexist views are often rein-
forced by the enabling responses of his victim. She attempts
to improve her relationship by ignoring her attacker's faults,
excusing them, and taking part of the blame for them.

Much of her time and energy are spent trying to justify
his violence against her and protect him from consequences.
When he goes on a drunk, she doctors him until he sobers
up. When he misses work as a result of a hangover, she

calls his boss with made-up excuses. When he has no money, she borrows it and gives it to him. When he is arrested for beating her, she often drops the charges because she doesn't want to hurt him.

Any time she fails to support him in any way, she feels a deep sense of guilt and fear.

Her batterer, of course, is well aware of her guilt feelings and knows precisely how to push her buttons to get exactly what he wants. He knows when and how to use:

- intimidation
- self-pity
- affection
- fear.

His emotional attacks range from subtle sarcasm to open verbal threats of harm and death. Many a victim has said that if she adds the physical abuse and the emotional abuse together, his abuse of her is continuous.

A disturbing number of battered women report that they are forced into sexual relations with their husbands immediately after being severely beaten.

This should not be misunderstood as an act of apology or remorse. It is nothing less than rape.

It is sexual violence—a further attempt by the batterer to humiliate and dominate his partner.

> One victim said she knew never to resist her husband's sexual attacks. "Resistance would only provoke more beatings," she said. "When he forced me into having sex, he would call me 'bitch' or 'whore' and always remind me I was no good. I almost believed him."

He dominates her social activities and restricts her physical movements, limiting her ability to develop support systems and escape his control. He is very aware that a woman without resources is a woman without choices.

> Another victim testified that her batterer made it a point to never buy a second family car, even though he could

*well afford to, because he didn't want her to have any
freedom of movement. He kept both sets of car keys in
his pocket, even when he slept.*

*When she asked to use the car, he always quizzed her
as to where she was going, why, and how long she
planned to be gone. She found it less intimidating to
take the bus.*

If the batterer needs the money his wife can earn, he lets
her work outside the home. Usually, he severely limits such
work in a deliberate attempt to totally isolate and control
her.

Lacks insight and motivation

Serial Batterers and most Sporadic Batterers don't understand their own anger and aggression. This results in
their:

- lacking insight into themselves
- having no motivation to change
- not responding to therapy or counseling.

**This batterer has extreme difficulty in understanding or
talking about his feelings of inner confusion and rage.**

He does not realize that many emotions are fueling his
sense of rage.

- He is unable to tell the difference between guilt, hurt,
  inadequacy, and grief.
- He cannot separate feelings of anxiety, insecurity, failure, and rejection.
- He does not see that each emotion has distinct causes
  and characteristics of its own.
- He groups all his emotions together into the single
  emotion of anger.

People who understand their emotional conflicts can
learn to deal with them in healthy and worthwhile ways.

**But the batterer's conflicts always come out aggressively
in destructive and damaging acts.**

The batterer's lack of insight not only keeps him from dealing appropriately with his feelings of rage, it also keeps him from taking responsibility for his actions.

He justifies his violence by claiming he was provoked.

If he does not understand his aggression, it's easier to blame someone or some event outside himself.

An informal study was done with a group of 40 men who had pleaded guilty to beating their wives. Each man was asked to give one reason for beating his wife.

- All 40 of the men justified and minimized their violence.
- One said, "I was too drunk to remember."
- 39 men specifically mentioned external reasons for their rage.

Not one mentioned feeling hurt, anxious, inadequate, or insecure. Not one gave any other emotional or internal reason for his violence.

In addition to a complete lack of insight, these abusers lack the motivation to change. To want change, someone must first recognize and admit to having a problem.

The batterer admits to nothing. His life is spent blaming others.

As a result, he is unmotivated to look for help. Though he may cry or show what appears to be remorse, a closer look proves that the tears are nothing more than deliberate manipulation.

- He tries to manipulate his partner into staying in the relationship when she is preparing to leave it.
- He tries to influence a court system that is prepared to imprison him.

But when his partner returns to him and the court orders are lifted, he is certain to return to his old ways. If he attended therapy because it was part of a court-ordered agreement, he quickly drops out and resumes his abuse.

TREATMENT FOR SERIAL BATTERERS

For a long time, counselors and defense attorneys for batterers have been urging that men who beat women see a therapist for treatment.

The Serial Batterer is beyond a therapist's help.

As we have seen, almost all serial abusers have personality disorders.

In addition, many have the problem of alcohol and drug abuse. It's well known within the mental health field that the outlook for such people is very poor.

The outlook is even worse for a Serial Batterer who has several personality disorders—plus alcoholism or drug problems—plus a total lack of insight and motivation to change. The Serial Batterer is a hopeless case for even the most trained therapist.

One of the most manipulative of the defense strategies practiced by attorneys who represent batterers is to recommend counseling for these men, especially when it is used to avoid punishment. Not only is this batterer beyond treatment, but recommending counseling gives false hope to his victim. He agrees to enter treatment, so she agrees to go back to him, but this only allows the cycle of family violence to continue.

The ending of the relationship, not therapy for the man, should be the main focus. The life of a woman or her child may depend on it.

Behavioral similarities

Abuses drugs and alcohol

A probation officer asked a group of 40 women if they believed alcohol or drug use by their partners played a role in their being beaten, and 32 answered "yes." Of those 32 victims, 29 felt that stopping the substance abuse problem would stop the physical abuse.

The victim herself often asks the court to help the batter-er get help for his drinking or drug problem, which often proves to be a dangerous mistake.

Even though the relationship between substance abuse and domestic abuse is very high, *alcohol and drugs are not the cause of the violence.* A man who is likely to beat his part-ner has many of the same characteristics as a person who is likely to abuse alcohol or drugs:

- low self-esteem
- low tolerance for frustration
- a need for power.

Substance abuse is only one symptom out of many that make up the personality disorder of the Serial Batterer.

It's the total effect of all symptoms that leads to this man's being abusive. He does not regularly beat his wife because he's a drunk. He beats her because he has a personality disorder. I repeat:

Alcohol abuse is merely a symptom of his disorder.

Although most men who abuse women are likely to abuse alcohol and drugs, most substance abusers are not batterers.

Even when a man is drinking heavily, chances are he is not going to beat his partner if he doesn't also have a few symptoms associated with a personality disorder.

However, if he is a batterer, his abuse of alcohol or drugs is very likely to:

- make him more violent
- make him more dangerous
- make him inflict more serious injury on his victim—even kill her.

Alcohol and drugs reduce the assailant's already limited ability to keep his impulses in check.

They reduce his ability to *inhibit* or control his bad be-havior. As these substances take effect, his inhibitions are released. The rage that's always inside of him explodes uncontrollably.

The amount of rage that explodes may depend on which personality disorder he has and which drugs he's taken.

For example, if a Serial Batterer with more than one personality disorder takes both alcohol and diet pills, his aggression could be disastrous.

A report entitled "The Drunken Bum Theory of Wife-Beating" suggests that the batterer learns:
- he can more easily deny any responsibility for his violence by blaming it on alcohol
- others are more likely to excuse him for beating his wife when he's been drinking.

This report also points out how drinkers learn that others expect them to act differently depending on location. For example: A man who "lets loose" in a bar manages to control himself at a church wedding, even when he's had the same amount of alcohol.

Source: "The Drunken Bum Theory of Wife Beating" is a paper presented by Glenda Kaufman Kantor and Murray A. Straus at the National Alcoholism Forum Conference, San Francisco, August 24, 1986.

With the exception of the Serial Batterer who has an antisocial personality disorder, most men who drink and attack their wives and girlfriends at home would not consider doing so in a crowded restaurant.

Many batterers get drunk so they can justify their violence.

As someone once said, "The batterer doesn't beat his wife because he drinks, he drinks in order to beat his wife."

Even without alcohol, many batterers continue to beat their partners.

After Jack was found guilty of assaulting his wife, she was interviewed. She said that although he'd been sober for more than a year and attended three Alcoholics Anonymous meetings a week, he came home and beat her after each meeting.

If a major cause of battering were the batterer's release of his inhibitions by drinking, most men would be potential wife beaters.

The fact is, most men who drink alcohol do not react violently or aggressively.

When a batterer appears in court for terrorizing and brutalizing his partner, drunkenness is often his only defense. Unfortunately, his family, as well as his victim, buys into this outrageous defense.

That's because alcohol is often the only explanation for his unbelievable violence, and reasonable people need some explanation for what is otherwise unexplainable.

Defense attorneys cleverly use the drunkenness excuse:
- to convince a judge or a jury that something other than the defendant is responsible for a gruesome attack
- to demand that the court offer the batterer a chance to rehabilitate himself, instead of punishing him for his crimes.

"If you put him in jail," they say, "he will only come out worse."

- Forget that the defendant broke his victim's legs and arms.
- Forget that he stabbed her with a steak knife several times after sexually assaulting her.
- Forget that he mutilated and murdered his victim.

The defense always focuses on the same issue:

"It's not my client's fault that he did what he did. His drinking made him do it."

Juries and judges are asked to ignore the fact that a defendant has a long history of physical violence against the same victim. They are asked to ignore his history of beating her when she was eight months pregnant, and the fact that she was hospitalized at different times following his other assaults.

They are asked to ignore the fact that he was sober during many of the past attacks.

They are urged to focus only on the claim that he has a drinking problem.

A great deal of domestic violence occurs when the man has *not* been drinking or using drugs.

The man, not the alcohol, is responsible for his aggression. It's his personality disorder—together with the combination of characteristics that make up his personality disorder—which makes him aggressive.

Through his entire life he has learned to be ruthless. He has also learned that there are no consequences for his violent behavior.

He will continue to deny responsibility for his behavior until someone stops him.

The courts must stop allowing alcoholism and drug addiction to be used as a defense for the brutal beating of a woman.

Manipulates

The batterer is a skilled manipulator. When his wife or girlfriend finally decides she's had enough of his abuse, he knows how to lure her back into the relationship. He cries, pleads, begs, and resorts to his masterpiece of manipulation—the threat of suicide.

He convinces his victim that his blood will be on her hands.

The batterer has the ability to make his victim feel pity, guilt, and shame. When these tactics don't work, he turns to terror and intimidation. He harasses her by phone, sends threatening notes, and stalks her.

The manipulator is very aware of when to use pity and when to use fear in his attempts to force the response he wants.

If she leaves him, he promises "to get help" for his problems. If she returns, he quickly goes back on his promises and resumes his violence.

Exploits

The Serial Batterer, as well as many a Sporadic Batterer, is a parasite. He feeds off others, especially his wife or girlfriend and his family. He sucks from them whatever they have to give him, and he does so without feeling he needs to give anything back.

When he's out of a job, which is often, he gets money from his partner, even his children. Much of the money they give him goes toward gambling, cigarettes, and alcohol or drugs. He counts on his wife to take care of family needs such as food, rent, and utilities.

If his wife or girlfriend is out of his life for a while, he gets his parents and relatives to give him housing and money. He bounces from one relative to another, using their home and food without a thought of repayment.

This man bleeds his partner and family emotionally as well as financially. He absorbs them into his babyish games and keeps them in a constant state of confusion.

His family's daily existence revolves around feeding his never-ending needs and demands.

Responding to his demanding and explosive nature fills his family with anxiety and distress. They live on the edge of an emotional cliff, choosing to keep him calm rather than risk a greater crisis.

If he's arrested for beating his wife or girlfriend, he calls from jail and demands that she pay his bail. It's not unusual for the victim herself to hire the attorney to represent him. If she refuses, he turns to his parents, relatives, or close friends for assistance. He knows that if he shops around, he will be able to get a friend or family member to give him the help he needs or wants. Those around him, he believes, should meet his every desire.

He goes through life feeling entitled to complete love and attention, regardless of how bad his behavior is.

There is no limit to his feeling of entitlement.

Throws tantrums

Childish tantrums are one of the most common behaviors shown by the Serial Batterer. He reacts to emotions such as rejection, failure, grief, stress, and insecurity with childlike rage.

His tantrums range from verbal assaults to destruction of personal property. He also threatens suicide.

During the peak of his rage, he might bite his victim and smash her furniture, finally curling up in the corner of a room and crying hysterically.

Such tantrums are common among all habitual batterers, regardless of their specific personality disorders.

Loses jobs

Many Serial Batterers, depending on their particular personality disorders, are not capable of holding a job for long periods of time.

They might hold several different jobs over the course of a year. Or they might be unemployed for months at a time.

The batterer always claims he was unfairly fired or he quit because the job did not meet his standards. During his periods of unemployment, he becomes increasingly dependent on others for money, particularly his parents, family, and partner.

Has criminal record

The Serial Batterer often has a long history of crime. How long a history usually depends on the type of personality disorder the batterer has.

His arrests are commonly for criminal trespassing, criminal damage, assault, threats, disturbing the peace, carrying concealed weapons, and simple and aggravated battery.

These arrests are all related to aggression.

Is abusive before marriage

The Serial Batterer has a history of beating his partner early in their relationship. Many women find themselves being assaulted while they are dating. Others report being physically attacked on the honeymoon.

Slapping, pushing, grabbing, and showing extreme jealousy are some of the early signs of aggression.

These are *indirect* signs that are sometimes hard to recognize as aggression. However, once the batterer feels he has a secure relationship, his indirect aggression turns into outright violence.

If he beats his girlfriend early in a relationship, his abuse will only get worse. Aggression before marriage is an obvious and important sign of future violence.

Don't pass it off as harmless.

Has many abusive relationships

The Serial Batterer abuses many victims over many years of relationships. Often, his victims know that he beat his former wives or girlfriends. His criminal record frequently shows that other women have charged him in the past for physical abuse. It's not unusual for a single victim to charge him with domestic violence several times during the same year.

All **his future intimate relationships with women will be violent.**

His current victim is not the first, and she is definitely not his last.

Demeans his partner

The Serial Batterer feels so inadequate that he continually tries to prove he's in charge by demeaning or putting down his wife or girlfriend.

Between his physical attacks on her, he uses insults to

attack her character and her self-esteem. In public and in private he assaults her ego, constantly reminding her that she's stupid, ugly, and unworthy of love. He also convinces her that she is incapable of managing for herself, thereby ensuring that she won't try to leave him.

Keeps her under surveillance

The Serial Batterer watches his victim's every move. If she's not at home when he gets there, he wants to know where she's been and with whom. He checks up on her by phone, supervises her mail, and listens in on her conversations with others.

He keeps her under surveillance, managing her movements the same way a warden manages prisoners.

Isolates her from others

He makes every possible attempt to isolate her from family, friends, and any type of support. He knows that if he keeps her from developing close personal relationships and support systems, she's less likely to leave him.

He won't let her visit friends, use the car, or take part in activities where she will meet other people.

Interferes with her job

The Serial Batterer is very threatened by his partner's attempts to work outside the home. He knows that a job will give her financial independence as well as contacts with other people who might help her to leave him.

If she tries to find a job, he threatens to harm her if she doesn't stop looking. If she has a job, he harasses her in an attempt to get her fired.

He knows that if she loses her job, he regains control.

He makes threatening phone calls to her at work, sends her obscene letters, and stalks her on or near her workplace. If she leaves him, his harassment and threats get dramatically worse.

Uses weapons

The Serial Batterer uses knives, guns, and clubs in attacking his victim. He constantly reminds her that he has a weapon and will use it if necessary.

He frequently holds a gun to her head and to the heads of her children. When he's enraged he fires, sometimes as a warning to threaten his victim.

Sometimes he actually shoots her and the children.

His weapon of choice is a handgun.

Tortures and mutilates

The Serial Batterer mutilates and tortures his victim in the same manner that an enemy abuses a prisoner of war.

He burns her with cigarettes and beats her with clubs, intending to disfigure her. He holds hot irons to her face and body and cuts her with sharp objects. He throws acid in her face and forces loaded guns up her vagina.

In cases where he has murdered his victim, he has been known to mutilate her body by cutting off her head and other body parts.

Bites

He is often known to savagely bite his victim. Biting is such a primitive act of aggression that it reveals just how abnormal the personality of the Serial Batterer is.

During the peak of his childish tantrums, he uses his teeth as a weapon, piercing and tearing flesh from his partner's limbs and body. Frequently, a victim appears in court with scars and injuries from the batterer's bite.

Beats his pregnant partner

Many women report having been beaten by their husbands or boyfriends while pregnant.

He punches her in the stomach, knocks her down, and kicks her, intending to injure her and her unborn child.

**His outright efforts to kill the fetus are attempts to get
rid of any threat to the position he occupies as the center of
his victim's attention.**

Causes serious injury

The Serial Batterer injures his victim so badly that she
frequently requires medical attention or hospitalization. The
most common injuries he inflicts on her are bruises to her
face, blackened and swollen eyes, broken noses and cheek-
bones, split and swollen lips, and broken teeth.

Although many of his blows focus on her face, she also
suffers severe bruising and bone fractures of her body, arms,
and legs. If his brutality doesn't kill her, the internal injuries she receives can eventually do so, causing her extreme
pain and ongoing illness for years. It's not unusual for her
to receive puncture and gunshot wounds.

Many of the injuries he inflicts permanently disable her.

Repeats cycles of abuse

The Serial Batterer has an ongoing systematic pattern of
abusing his wife or girlfriend. Throughout their relationship, the same "phases" occur over and over in a predictable pattern.

Following a savage beating comes the "honeymoon
phase," in which the abuser:
- pretends he's sorry
- appears to be concerned—but only on the surface
- attempts to make up with her; for example, by bringing her flowers
- assures her that she is loved
- promises to never hurt her again.

Once he feels secure that he's managed to lure his victim
back into the relationship, he starts his pattern of abuse over
again. It, too, is followed by the same "honeymoon phase"
in a never-ending cycle.

Intimidates and terrorizes

The Serial Batterer intimidates and terrorizes his victim in an effort to frighten her into submission. His terrorism might range from telephone threats to open stalking, including physical assaults with loaded weapons.

His actions are designed to force her back into the relationship after she has left and to maintain control while they are together.

Like his physical attacks, the terrorism is systematic, habitual, and ongoing. It often succeeds in making his victim feel completely helpless.

Stalks

Stalking is one of the most intense forms of intimidation.

It's violence from a distance—an undercover method of maintaining control.

Without speaking a word, the stalker shows his victim how easy it would be to kill her. He lets his victim see him sitting across from her house doing nothing more than watching her. He follows her on foot and with his car. He rides past her house over and over again. He hides and watches from the shadows of the night. He hides himself behind shrubbery and buildings.

If he sees her going out with friends, especially boyfriends, his stalking often turns into a violent physical confrontation.

"I was like a prisoner of war," Jane reports. "He censored my mail, my phone calls, even my conversations with my mom and dad. He followed me to work and frequently surprised me by coming home in the middle of the day. On one occasion I noticed him hiding in the woods behind our house. On another, I found him hiding in the trunk of my car. I had a flat tire as I drove to work, and as I went to get my spare, there he was.

"We have since separated," Jane adds, "but he continues to stalk me. I went to the police but they said that until my divorce is final, he has certain rights. What about my rights?"

Harasses

The Serial Batterer's intimidation and harassment are worst during periods of estrangement. He calls his victim on the phone endlessly, alternating between hysterical pleadings and threats of suicide. When neither works, he threatens her with violence and death.

Many batterers make 30 to 50 harassing calls a day.

One victim logged as many as 300 calls during the course of a week. Although she had her phone number changed, the calls started up again.

Another form of harassment is sending letters through the mail. The batterer also places notes on his victim's car windshield and attaches them to the door of her house. Like the phone calls, his messages range from emotional pleadings to threats of violent retaliation.

Damages his partner's property

The Serial Batterer not only systematically batters his partner's face and body but also repeatedly damages and destroys her personal property, particularly her car.

He breaks furniture, kicks in the television, and pulls phone cords from the wall. He rips and burns his victim's clothes and smashes windows and mirrors.

Most of the damage he does occurs after she tries to get out of the relationship. It is both a form of revenge and an attempt to keep her from running away.

He slashes her tires and throws bricks through her windshield. He opens her hood and ruins the engine and wiring. He cuts the seats and interior with a knife and sets her car on fire.

Damage to a vehicle is one of the most commonly reported acts of the batterer's vandalism. It is also one of the most difficult to prove.

His destruction of her car is symbolic of his desire to destroy her.

Kidnaps the children

When a woman leaves a Serial Batterer, it's not unusual for him to kidnap her children. He forces his way into her house, grabs the children, makes them get into his car, and speeds away. Then he phones her and uses the children as a bargaining chip to force his victim back into a relationship.

He is very aware that terrorized and terrified children are his best means of getting his estranged partner to return.

Can commit murder

Most Serial Batterers do not kill their wives or girlfriends—just as most alcoholics don't kill others when they drive. But we have to think about what *might* happen.

In the same way that the habitual drinker is capable of killing on the highway, the habitual batterer is capable of killing in the home.

Of all homicides in this country, according to the Bureau of Justice Statistics, nearly 15 percent involve family or intimate relationships. The total number in a 10-year period is nearly equal to the number of American military casualties that occurred over the 10 years we were at war in Vietnam.

Some murders committed by husbands and boyfriends are spontaneous, but many are well planned ahead of time.

In any relationship with a batterer, the potential for him to kill his partner is always there.

Can harm others

The Serial Batterer is capable of mass murder. He's a potential threat to everyone who gets in his way, especially when he believes they are helping or influencing his wife or girlfriend to leave him.

He frequently injures or kills her parents, children, friends, roommates, and new boyfriends. There is perhaps no time in which he is more dangerous than during periods in which they are separated from each other.

Summary

- According to remarkably similar details reported by victims, batterers have a great many emotions and behaviors in common.
- Recognizing the warning signs can help keep a woman from getting into a relationship with a batterer. He does not improve after marriage.
- These similarities help us to determine where a batterer falls on the Batterer's Continuum and to predict how dangerous he will continue to be to his victim.
- Serial Batterers and most Sporadic Batterers do not change. They continue to deny responsibility for their violence, to minimize the damage they have done, to blame situations outside themselves, such as alcohol or drugs, and to find excuses for behaving as they do.
- They show no remorse, no ability to bond with others, and no capacity to love anyone. Usually, they dislike themselves intensely.
- Often, they display an exciting emotional intensity that attracts others to them.
- Many of their possessive behaviors, such as making a woman dependent on them, reveal their own dependency.
- They have no insight and no motivation to change. The vast majority of them are beyond treatment.

PART II

HELPING WOMEN FIND SAFE PASSAGE FROM ABUSIVE RELATIONSHIPS

Chapter 7

Stop the Battering

"It's been a long, hard journey," Linda writes after ultimately leaving Bob, a violent and abusive husband, "but I have finally been able to get my life back on track. I was able to accomplish this with the help of many resources.

"I now have a very good job in the legal department of a large company, and I'm getting to the point that I can have the things I want. Most valuable of all, I have some peace in my life."

There are two ways to look at stopping the dreadful cycle of abuse. One is political, the other, personal.

In this book I do not deal with political change, which involves large-scale efforts to make changes in society.

Instead I deal with personal action—the kind that any woman, as well as her friends and family, can learn to take to protect her safety and the safety of her children.

Personal action benefits the person who takes that action; political action benefits future generations, sometimes not until long after the death of the individuals who started doing something to bring about the change.

POLITICAL ACTION

Large-scale efforts to change society come about over time, as great numbers of people agree that certain evils, such as violence against women, shall no longer be tolerated.

These large-scale changes are known as political because they involve changes in power, such as the power men have over women. To change this power means working to:

- eliminate the causes of male aggression
- change the social systems that accept male aggression as normal—for example, judges who dismiss charges against rapists because they have the attitude that "boys will be boys."

Social systems are slow to change, even when most people agree that change must take place.

Changing or balancing the power some people have over others involves nothing less than major cultural shifts—that is, a change in attitudes, parenting methods, the mass media, education, law enforcement and the criminal justice system, employment, access to money and other resources, and religious teachings—to name just a few of our social institutions that bear some share of responsibility for allowing the widespread abuse of women and children to continue.

Someone who wants to bring about a change in any of these major areas does not have to tackle all of them, or do so alone. Many organizations exist for the sole purpose of focusing efforts on making specific changes in specific social institutions. You can learn about some of these action organizations through a domestic violence program or by looking in a directory of organizations at your local library.

The beneficiaries of political and social action are our daughters, granddaughters, great-granddaughters.

Personal action anyone can take

The most important action anyone can take is to see that the woman who is being beaten by a man is *safe*. Often, this means one or more of the following actions:

- getting the batterer to stop the beating by seeing that he gets some form of therapy
- getting the batterer put away by seeing that the police and the courts take action
- getting the woman and her children away from the batterer, either temporarily or permanently.

In other words: he changes, he is locked up, or the woman leaves.

What if you feel that taking any kind of action is too hard for you? It's not unusual to feel that way if you are the one who is frequently beaten, terrorized, and kept isolated from others. You probably feel helpless and hopeless.

That's just how your batterer wants you to feel.

- But you don't have to do everything alone.
- And you don't have to do everything at once.

I will be honest with you: it won't be easy, and it might not show results right away. At times it might seem that for every two steps forward you take, circumstances push you back a step. *But that's still a step forward.*

For many women, ending their abuse means ending their relationships. You might not feel comfortable with that decision. In fact, you might not feel comfortable with the idea of making any decision at this time.

Of course, deciding to do nothing is also a decision.

What you do to stop being beaten depends on two things:

1. What *you* are ready for.
2. What kind of batterer *he* is.

The women whose stories I am sharing with you throughout this book also went through periods of self-doubt and despair similar to what you might be feeling right now. Each wondered, as you might be doing:

- "What can *I* do?"
- "What can *anybody* do?"

The answer is: One person can save one woman's life.

Believe you'll succeed

Anyone who wants change to occur first needs to *believe it will happen*.

There are two techniques you can use to be successful. Athletes and performers use these techniques all the time to reach their goals: *visualization* and *affirmation*.

- Visualization: The woman who wants to live a safe, healthy life needs a *vision* of herself actually living that better life.
- Affirmation: She has to replace the negative failure messages in her head with positive "I can do it" messages, so she gets herself to *really* believe in herself and her ultimate success.

Authors who specialize in teaching these very effective techniques have produced some fine books and audiocassette tapes for women. These materials tell you just how to go about creating the kind of mental environment that empowers you to change your life, even when you don't think you can—or should. Ask at your local library or bookstore for help in finding these resources.

By learning techniques such as visualization and affirmation, you can build the determination you need to carry you through the process of making change in your life.

Believe in your support system

You aren't in this alone, although your batterer might have succeeded in getting you to feel alone.

- Family and friends can help you.
- Agencies in your community can help you.
- Support groups and battered women's programs exist to help you.

Executive wives and professional women who are battered feel especially alone. Like most people, each of these women thinks violence in the home happens only to "other women."

This victim's isolation is increased by her marriage to a prominent man in the community. She fears his power and influence will make it impossible for her to go to the authorities or confide in anyone. She might be telling herself, "If I'm so smart that I reached this status in life, how could I let this happen to me? I'm not what I pretend to be, and I must keep others from discovering how phony I really am."

In addition, she feels shamed and humiliated. She thinks she'll "die of embarrassment" if she goes to a battered women's shelter.

If she doesn't go, she could die for real.

No woman has to be alone. Whether you are the victim or a member of her family, a friend of hers, or an individual who simply wants to help, the rest of this book tells you:
- what treatment can and cannot do
- how the law enforcement system works
- what community programs to look for
- how to build a support system and create a safety plan.

I describe in detail three strategies for personal action:
1. Getting the abuser involved in a treatment and rehabilitation program, if appropriate for him.
2. Making sure the criminal justice system is taking all the steps it is supposed to.
3. Creating a personal safety plan that enables the woman to leave her abuser, either temporarily or permanently.

These actions are choices. You can act on any one method, any two methods, or all three.

The goal is to stop the battering.

Before we begin, the victim of a batterer needs to know:

- Just because you are about to learn what you can do to end your abuse does *not* mean that you are in any way to blame for that abuse.
- You do not have to spend the rest of your life as a punching bag for your partner, forced to watch your children threatened, terrorized, and taught that violence is "normal."
- No one can help you more than you are willing to help yourself.

I was speaking before a group of health care professionals at a local conference on domestic violence, and as I looked into the audience, I made eye contact with an attractive woman in a nurse's uniform. I was certain we had met before, but I couldn't place her.

During my talk, she asked several questions that led me to believe she had been a victim. As the program ended, she and a younger woman came up to me. Both were smiling.

The older woman said, "You're probably wondering who we are. My name is Mary and this is my daughter Melanie. I'm the woman from Texas you helped many years ago when we came to New Orleans to get away from my boyfriend.

"I wanted you to know that we're safe and doing fine," she said. "The steps we took after running away many years ago probably saved our lives. We stayed here, knowing that if we were to remain safe, we had to stay where we had a support system."

Suddenly I had a vivid flashback of Mary and her three small girls huddling in a stairwell at the courthouse many years before. I had encountered them as I'd left my office at the end of a busy work week. Mary had what appeared to be her belongings jammed into a supermarket shopping cart, and the children were shabbily dressed. They had no place to go and no money. The night before, they'd slept in the back of a church; the night before that, in an abandoned office building.

I recalled having driven them to a shelter for the weekend. On Monday morning when I'd arrived at work, I'd been surprised to see the family waiting to see me. Mary's right eye had been swollen shut and the left severely bruised.

Mary hadn't known that her brutal boyfriend had followed her and her three girls from Texas, even though she'd told no one where she was going, not even her family. The weekend she stayed at the shelter, she and the girls had gone to a nearby park for a change of scenery. Her abuser had come up behind her as she sat on a park bench and knocked her to the ground.

"He began to grab my throat with both hands and beat my head against the sidewalk," Mary had told me the day after her attack. Melanie had tried to pull him off as the two younger girls ran for the police. He had tried to run, but the officers had caught up with him and brought him to jail. When Mary had come to my office that Monday morning, it was to see what I could do to keep him behind bars.

As Mary now stood before me in her white nurse's uniform, she said, "I wanted you to know that what you, the police, the courts, and the shelter did for us back then worked. It certainly made my ex-boyfriend leave us alone. After he got out of jail, he left New Orleans and never returned." She went on to say, "The shelter you referred me to placed me in an educational program, and then I enrolled in nursing school. I graduated last year and have a job attending to battered women. I feel I have been blessed. My daughter Melanie recently enrolled in the same program."

We hugged, and I sensed the woman's peace.

"Again, we want to thank you," said Mary. "The help I got back then worked. It really helped change my life."

The lives of four people—Mary and her three daughters—had been given a new beginning because she got the help she needed.

But it happened only because she had been willing to take three essential steps.

1. She had the willingness to leave an abusive relationship and save herself and her children.
2. She had the determination to follow through and seek the help she needed to put her batterer in jail.
3. She had the vision to get the job training she needed to make a good life for herself and her children.

> **The rural woman is doubly isolated. In addition to her batterer's cutting her off from family and friends, community services may not be available.**
>
> **The belief that "everyone knows everyone else" in the small community makes the abused woman even more reluctant to seek help from local law enforcement and medical personnel.**
>
> **This is all the more reason to get information about the nearest resources by using the toll-free hotlines listed on page 219.**

Summary

- The goal is to stop the battering and help the woman find safe passage from the abusive relationship.
- Whether you are the woman being battered or someone in a position to help her, consider these three strategies for personal action: treating the batterer, prosecuting him, or leaving him.
- The strategy to use depends on the category of batterer and on the woman's situation.
- No one has to do it alone. Many resources exist to help women build a support system.

Chapter 8

Treating the Batterer

"When we first met I thought Joe was the most charming man in the world. He lit my cigarettes and pulled my chair out for me as I sat down. He seemed so very confident, considerate, and conscientious. He flattered and complimented me to the point of seduction."

Only a month into their relationship, Kim began to realize that Joe was a phony. "I'm disturbed I didn't recognize him for what he was the night we met," she told her counselor. "Looking back, I now realize he had been very controlling and superficial. He didn't ask me for a date, he demanded it. And when he learned I had other plans, he saw that I broke them.

"One night as we were dressing for a party, he questioned me as to why I no longer found him attractive. He insisted that I'd probably prefer going to the party with someone else. As I tried to reassure him, he went crazy, cutting up my party dress with a knife and threatening suicide. It was then that he threw me on the floor, grabbed a mop handle, broke it, and shoved it up my vagina. As I bled profusely, he began to sob hysterically, falling to the floor and pleading for forgiveness. He curled up in the corner of the room, and I cradled him in my arms. You would have thought he was the one who'd been attacked," said Kim.

"It took me two years," Kim added, "but I finally left him. I felt so guilty and responsible for his condition. I thought I could change him. What a fool I was."

To stop the battering, the kind of action that comes to mind for many people is to change the batterer's attitudes. Getting him into some kind of treatment program is expected to change his thinking about his behavior toward the women in his life and give him healthier ways of handling his anger.

Let's consider the effectiveness of this kind of action by looking at what kinds of treatment are available and how appropriate they are for different batterers.

Types of treatment

Treatment can include any number of methods, ranging from individual counseling by a trained and credentialed psychotherapist to support groups led by volunteer nonprofessionals. It can include spiritual counseling and marriage counseling.

Individual or one-on-one counseling

The Serial Batterer (Category 3): Treatment is not encouraged, as we've already discussed and will discuss again.

The Sporadic Batterer (Category 2): For some of these batterers who appear sincerely motivated to change, one kind of treatment recommended is individual counseling. It allows the batterer to:

- focus on the roots of his aggression
- gain insight into the flawed personality characteristics that fuel his rage.

Such counseling should give the batterer a private way of exploring his feelings of inadequacy, self-doubt, low self-esteem, and so on.

Although counseling might bring out the fact that he was a victim himself, it must not allow him to use his past victimization as an excuse for his current behavior.

The Remorseful Batterer (Category 1): He has the highest likelihood of benefiting from individual counseling, but it's important that the counselor he sees be a *specialist*.

That's because his isolated episode of violent behavior was related to his feelings about a particular traumatic event in his life. It could have been a catastrophe he didn't know how to handle, or it could represent the beginning of a drinking or drug problem.

If the batterer had a heart problem, he would see a heart specialist. If he had cancer, he would see a cancer specialist. Likewise:

- If his violence is related to grief, he should see a counselor who specializes in grief therapy.
- If his rage is related to stress, he should see a counselor who specializes in stress.
- If he has a drinking or drug problem, he should enter a substance abuse program.

Unless the Category 1 batterer deals with the *specific* problems that caused him to become violent, his rage and related violence are likely to continue.

Group counseling

Group counseling is a lower-cost method of treating many batterers at the same time. It can reduce treatment costs by as much as 75 percent, allowing more batterers to get the counseling they need, which they might not otherwise be able to afford.

For the *Sporadic Batterer,* group counseling is strongly recommended in addition to individual counseling. That's because group counseling:

- reinforces what he learns about himself through individual counseling
- gives him a setting in which the therapist and members of the group can appropriately confront his ideas about power and control, the roles of men and women, and traditional sexist attitudes

- helps him unlearn and change many of the harmful behaviors he learned because of his upbringing
- helps him learn communication skills, stress reduction skills, and anger management, giving him a sense of control over his own behavior by giving him some of the tools he needs to stop his own violence.

One problem of group counseling is that members of the group can sometimes reinforce each other's harmful ideas and behaviors.

But counselors who are used to working with batterers are able to recognize and prevent such effects.

Support groups

For the *Remorseful Batterer* and the *Sporadic Batterer,* support groups offer these benefits:

- They enable the batterer to build relationships with others who have the same problems.
- They develop a sense of fellowship. This in itself can reduce the batterer's feelings of being alone, and, for the Sporadic Batterer, help him establish his identity.
- They are especially good for men who are also in individual counseling, since they help to fill the time between individual counseling sessions.
- Most are free. Most groups are also easily available, depending on the type of support most suited to the batterer's problem.

Remorseful Batterers get the most from attending support groups that focus on the specific areas that give them trouble.

For example, a support group for people overcome by the death of a loved one gives the grieving batterer contact with others who are also experiencing grief and who can relate to his pain. If his aggression is due to drinking or the use of drugs, either Alcoholics Anonymous (AA) or Narcotics Anonymous (NA) is recommended. Such groups are available in almost every city in the country.

Sporadic Batterers should also attend meetings of AA or Narcotics Anonymous if they have been diagnosed with alcoholism or drug addiction. Such groups should be thought of as part of an effective treatment program, and never as the total solution to the batterer's problem.

Whereas alcohol and other drugs might increase this man's aggression and make his violence more deadly, these substances do not cause his aggression.

Thus, treatment for substance abuse alone is unlikely to stop his violence.

The support groups appropriate for a Sporadic Batterer should confront his behavior and reinforce what he is learning about himself in individual and group counseling.

Joint counseling

As its name indicates, this type of counseling involves both partners in therapy together. Joint counseling is also called *marriage counseling.*

Usually, a therapist should not suggest joint counseling in matters of domestic abuse.

But in cases of Category 1 violence, joint counseling may be appropriate. It's especially appropriate if the woman decides to stay in the relationship. Joint counseling can help both partners deal with:

- the roots of this batterer's aggression
- the emotional wounds it causes to his partner.

When partners agree to deal with these issues together in joint counseling, that does *not* mean the victim of a Remorseful Batterer is to blame for the man's violence.

It *does* provide the woman with an opportunity to:

- understand his rage
- deal with her own fears, apprehension, and emotional scars, and
- decide the direction she should take in her relationship with him.

In cases of Category 2 violence, therapists generally agree that joint counseling, marriage counseling, or family counseling are not appropriate and don't work.

In addition, putting the Sporadic Batterer in a joint counseling situation together with the target of his aggression:

- assumes that the man and woman are on an equal footing and are a match for each other—which is not true
- implies, perhaps, that his victim shares some of the blame for his violence—which is also not true
- allows the batterer to continue to dominate the woman, leading her to mistrust and avoid all counseling in the future
- places her in a situation in which she is afraid to talk about her worries and concerns, knowing that doing so could lead to another beating.

If you are a woman being battered by a Serial Batterer or a Sporadic Batterer, be prepared for people who advise you that he "should get help" for his problems, and that you should join him in therapy.

You could even get a call from the batterer's therapist recommending joint counseling.

Often, the expectation in joint counseling is one of getting you back together again with your abuser.

Look at such advice with distrust.

Spiritual counseling

The spiritual needs of Category 1 and 2 batterers should not be ignored. It is not by chance that Alcoholics Anonymous promotes the spiritual side of an alcoholic's efforts to rehabilitate himself. AA uses a nondenominational approach in recognizing a person's instinctive need for spiritual guidance.

If the batterer has spiritual leanings, it's appropriate to encourage him to see his priest, minister, rabbi, or other advisor.

This does not mean that a minister should become a mediator between the batterer and his victim, or that spiritual counseling can take the place of psychotherapy.

The suggestion simply offers one additional means for the batterer to meet his needs.

Counseling and treatment for the woman

If you have a relationship with a Remorseful Batterer, you might want to consider individual counseling for yourself to help you deal with your own needs—whether or not you stay in your relationship.

If you are in a relationship with a batterer who is also a substance abuser or an alcoholic, you can get additional support by regularly attending meetings of Al-Anon, a support group for family members of alcohol and drug abusers.

If you are in a relationship with a Serial or Sporadic Batterer, definitely consider individual counseling for your own peace of mind and for personal growth as you prepare for a healthier future.

How willing is he to get therapy?

Remorseful Batterers usually are genuinely sorry for their violence and are sincerely motivated to get treatment for their problems.

Hence, treatment for these batterers is often successful.

If a Remorseful Batterer resists getting therapy, he might have to be forced into it. But the effort could be worthwhile.

If the batterer has been criminally charged, you can ask the judge or prosecutor handling the case to have the court order him into a qualified treatment program. If necessary, let your partner know you will leave if he does not get therapy.

Serial Batterers don't enter treatment because of any desire to change. It's because they want control. Once they have it, they drop out of treatment almost immediately and go right back to their criminal behavior.

The victim of a Serial Batterer must resist all attempts by him or others to involve her in his therapy.

The Serial Batterer's lack of insight into his rage, his extreme denial, and his total lack of motivation to change make him a clinical nightmare for even the most qualified therapist. Although I support treatment for certain batterers, experience shows that treatment for Serial Batterers has been a failure.

Some men can learn to change their behavior; others cannot. The difference is crucial.

Sporadic Batterers seldom enter treatment unless they are forced to, and they usually remain in treatment only until they have manipulated their partners back into the relationship. They present special challenges.

Motivation

How can you tell when a particular Sporadic Batterer is different enough from a Serial Batterer that he becomes a possible candidate for treatment and rehabilitation?

There's no absolute way to measure:

- whether his remorse is real or fake
- whether his tears show compassion for his partner or he's just trying to manipulate the situation
- whether his motivation to change is genuine or false.

However, there are ways to *test* this man's sincerity. No batterer puts up with therapy over a long period of time unless he's sincere about wanting to change. Therefore, if he's not sincere, he'll demonstrate this himself by dropping out without completing the program.

Time is your ally.

If he drops out, he is almost certain to batter again. When he does turn violent, you have to be prepared to end the relationship.

> **Be sure that in ending a relationship with a batterer, you use a support system and safety plan. These are described in Chapter 12.**

If the Sporadic Batterer successfully finishes a program, there's hope. In general, the more complete the treatment program, the more likely he is to change. If the program is not extensive, it's likely his violence will continue.

The threat of jail might not be the best way to get the Sporadic Batterer to *begin* feeling motivated, but it *is* usually effective in making any motivation he already has more intense.

Types of treatment

For a Sporadic Batterer to change his behavior, it's essential that his treatment include all of the following:
- individual therapy
- group therapy
- a strong support group.

Therapy deals with deeply rooted emotional and psychological problems. It increases the batterer's insight into himself, which is necessary for his rehabilitation.

Support groups are made up of people who have similar problems. They include groups such as:
- Alcoholics Anonymous
- Batterers Anonymous

The Sporadic Batterer is *not* likely to change if:
- he has a support group but does not regularly participate in therapy
- he attends therapy but is without a support group.

That's because each type of treatment has its limits. Although support groups fill an essential purpose, they should never be seen as a substitute for individual and group therapy.

Let me share two basic realities of therapy:

1. The cost of individual counseling makes it unlikely that a counselor will spend more than two hours a week with any one batterer—probably less. This is *not* enough time for a Sporadic Batterer to explore the insights he is learning and to see how he might change. During the rest of his week, he has quite a gap during which he has no outside support.

   If he is to keep his anger under control, he must develop a strong safety net to carry him through the periods between therapy.

   That's what the meetings of regular support groups accomplish.

2. The second reality is that most support groups are not able to deal with the Sporadic Batterer's many psychological problems. Nor are they designed to.

   Support groups are excellent for:

   a) allowing the batterer to let out his feelings and emotions

   b) revealing to him useful alternatives to physical violence.

Addictions

Groups such as Alcoholics Anonymous and Batterers Anonymous offer especially useful methods to help the individual to:

- deal with addictions
- figure out who he is and begin to build a sense of identity
- develop ways of controlling his impulses
- reduce his feelings of being isolated from people.

It's common for a Sporadic Batterer to stop drinking but keep abusing his partner.

At meetings of Alcoholics Anonymous, such a man is called a "dry drunk." This means he's managed to stop drinking but hasn't dealt with his deeper problems—whatever is making him feel inadequate or insecure. When his insecure feelings return, he behaves in all the ways he's addicted to—such as punching his wife and terrorizing his children—even though he might be "dry" when it comes to the bottle.

Such behaviors are far worse than being drunk.

The fact is, unless a sober batterer also deals with his deeper psychological conflicts through professional counseling, he will almost certainly continue to batter.

If a Sporadic Batterer enters treatment, it's essential for him to recognize that his abuse of his wife or girlfriend, and his abuse of alcohol or drugs, are two different problems.

He must never be allowed to excuse his violence by blaming his drinking.

> **Most people who abuse alcohol or drugs in our society never physically attack their mates. Drinking does not necessarily lead to battering. Each problem is a separate area for rehabilitation.**

The batterer first needs to deal with his problem of using mind-altering substances.

Otherwise, he never gets the stability he needs for dealing with his psychological problems and related violence.

In addition, it's essential for therapists to recognize the difference between the batterer's violence and his addiction to alcohol or drugs. Too often, therapists see the two problems as one. So they focus on using their methods for treating addictive personalities.

Although many of those treatment methods help the batterer become sober, they often fail miserably at dealing with the inner problems that cause his aggression.

Putting a batterer in a treatment program for drug or alcohol abuse gives false hope to his partner about his becoming a changed man. False hope puts her in greater danger.

IN THESE SITUATIONS...	TAKE THESE STEPS...
If the partner of a Sporadic Batterer is thinking of staying in the relationship...	She should physically separate from him until he has been in treatment at least six months. She should deny all requests to return to him before the agreed-upon time.
If he's been charged with a crime that does not require his being jailed...	The judge should reset his case for a hearing each month for at least one year. The judge should make him show proof of his being in therapy.
If he belongs to a support group...	The judge should make him bring his sponsor to court.
If his wife or girlfriend is still in a relationship with him...	She should appear in court to confirm his claims of treatment and to verify that he has not continued to abuse her.

Outlook for success

It's not promising. The Sporadic Batterer often has many of the characteristics of the Serial Batterer. He lacks motivation to change and is potentially homicidal as well.

Hence, I am *not* attempting to convince the victim of a Sporadic Batterer to stay in a relationship with her abuser. I am trying to be objective about the possibilities of treatment for this man when there are so many different theories about how to treat him.

When good people give bad advice

Most people never give any thought to the important differences among batterers. If you are in a violent relationship, you are likely to hear a lot of advice about getting counseling for an abuser who might be absolutely the worst candidate for it.

This advice might come from family and friends, from professionals in the criminal justice system, and from practitioners who offer one or more types of treatment.

Let's look at some of the advice to watch out for.

Treatment advice

If you are seeking guidance from family, friends, or even professionals because the man who claims to love you is physically assaulting you, many of these very caring individuals are likely to recommend that you stay with this man and help him get treatment for his problems.

"After all," they might say to convince you, "he must have problems to do what he does."

They perceive him to be a victim in his own right, a man who is not personally responsible for his rage and violence. They excuse his behavior because it's related to bad childhood experiences, to drinking, or to circumstances beyond his control.

These caring advisors might suggest that you go with your batterer to see your minister or a marriage counselor. Or that you get the batterer into AA or some other treatment program while you attend Al-Anon for the families of alcoholics.

Is this good advice? It depends.

The advice is probably good if your batterer fits the description of a Remorseful Batterer or a *very limited number of Sporadic Batterers*. Treatment can be beneficial if all three of the following are true:

- if he feels real remorse for his isolated act of violence
- if he's motivated to change
- if he doesn't represent a significant danger to you.

But if your batterer fits the description of a Serial Batterer, such advice could get you seriously injured or killed.

You are better off running for your life—after creating a personal safety plan to protect you from his coming after you.

Be guided by what you are learning about the three different categories of batterers and what you know of the batterer who is victimizing you.

When you get bad advice from good people, it can be awkward to ignore their suggestions, especially when you are asking for their help. So it helps to recognize that the society in which we live:

- puts a lot of faith in treatment as the solution to all family problems
- believes that preserving the family unit is always better than breaking it up
- thinks that a somewhat violent family is better than no family at all.

Someone who thinks all batterers are alike and should all get treatment doesn't want to believe that there's no cure for the batterer—even the many thousands of men who ruthlessly exploit and control their wives and girlfriends, and *who know right from wrong but just don't care.*

Someone who promotes treatment for a man who fits the profile of a Serial Batterer is no wiser than someone who promotes treatment for serial rapists and serial killers.

You might find a misguided advisor very hard to resist as he or she tries to convince you that treatment is the humane and appropriate thing to do—even though there's plenty of evidence to show that *treatment for Serial Batterers doesn't work.*

It doesn't work because these cold and vicious abusers feel no responsibility for their violent behavior, no remorse for the injuries they inflict, and no motivation to change. They pretend to be interested in treatment, but only until they succeed in manipulating their victims back into the relationship.

Regrettably, if you are the victim of a Serial Batterer, you are having to deal with two very difficult situations:

1. surviving the abuse, humiliation, and destruction of your self-esteem by this monstrous man in your life

2. resisting the very persuasive arguments of those who believe all individuals have an absolute right to treatment, regardless of the brutality of their crimes.

Such arguments for treatment are reasonable in instances of Category 1 violence and in *some* instances of Category 2 violence. However, they are unacceptable in instances of Category 3 violence and in most instances of Category 2 violence.

Don't be persuaded by the argument that "jail will only make him worse."

If the Serial Batterer isn't in jail, he is continuing to abuse women.

It's distressing to realize that many professionals—therapists, clergy, lawyers, judges, and others—would rather gamble on exposing you to more violence than risk appearing insensitive to the needs of men who are troubled or have "family problems."

If you are the victim of a man who is capable of habitual violence, you need to be on guard not only against your batterer, but also against those who sincerely believe that trying to cure a severely disturbed abuser is in your best interest.

Such well-meaning folks reason that the way to stop domestic violence is to help the batterer deal with the cause of his violence. In the process, you, your friends, and your family could all be murdered as you sit around your dinner table.

Here are several other reasons your advisors might be giving you bad information:

- They might never have had guns held to their heads or been terrorized or tortured, so they cannot really know how strong your fear is or how dangerous your abuser can be.
- They might assume that alcohol and drugs are causing the beatings and believe that treating the substance abuse will end the violence.

- They often see all batterers as being one and the same, and therefore they give the same advice to all victims, regardless of the batterer's individual personality disorders or extremes of brutality and ruthlessness.
- They might try to represent both of you at the same time, biasing themselves by wanting to both rehabilitate the batterer and keep your relationship together.
- They might be taken in by the charm that the batterer pours on whenever he wants to manipulate others for his purpose.

For women being abused by Serial Batterers and most Sporadic Batterers, it can be very dangerous to accept the advice of those who recommend treatment for a ruthless brute who has no conscience. Getting such abusers involved in a treatment and rehabilitation program gives hope to victims that their batterers will change.

Hope can give a woman a false sense of security and leave her open to further violence.

Just as serious, the victim's agreeing to treatment for the Serial Batterer simply gives back to him what he most desires, control.

He might start a treatment program. He won't finish it.

Instead, by entering treatment, the Serial Batterer:

- gets to manipulate his victim back into the relationship
- is given the means to persuade a court to drop charges against him.

You are already a victim. You don't need to be further victimized by well-meaning but poor advice.

Spiritual advice

Religious institutions place a great emphasis on the preservation of the family. As you attempt to address your batterer's violence, you might be faced with the conflict between what your religion teaches as being spiritually correct, and what you know is essential to your physical safety.

Although ending a marriage could go against your religious convictions, I strongly recommend it in cases of repeated violence.

You must recognize the real danger you are in. Separate your personal safety needs from your religious teachings.

I urge you to challenge any spiritual advisor who promotes the religious belief that it's wrong to leave the man who beats you. Seriously question the wisdom of those who want you to believe it's your responsibility to keep the family together through spiritual intervention. Many devout believers have accepted such advice and gone to their graves trying. Prayer and faith alone will not stop a Serial Batterer from his violent and ungodly viciousness.

I'm not suggesting that if your minister, priest, or rabbi insists on your entering into spiritual counseling with your batterer, you must stop practicing your religion. If, however, the advice you receive conflicts with your personal safety, consider separating your spiritual needs from those involving your spouse.

Seek counseling from an agency that can be more objective.

"The man I married was a professional with a high security clearance," explains Donna. "He was charming, evil, and incapable of connecting emotionally with anyone, except on the surface.

"It was a second marriage for us both, and we spent endless sessions with ministers and therapists to help work things out between us.

"One minister told me to pray and leave my independent ways at the office. The therapist told me to pack up and get out before it was too late.

"Eventually I accepted the idea of leaving. I was fortunate; no one was killed."

Partners in crime

It is not that treatment for batterers should be discouraged. In fact, the treatment of men who are legitimately remorseful and motivated to change must always be encouraged. It's only that we must learn to differentiate between those who feel a sense of responsibility for what they have done and those who are without a conscience.

Only by assessing each batterer individually can we be certain that when we advocate for treatment, such a choice is the correct path in the particular situation.

Though the rage of these individuals is generally linked to early environmental deprivation and horrendous childhood experiences, so is the rage of the serial killer.

What is it that we owe men who systematically terrorize and brutalize their wives and girlfriends? Why is it we continue to excuse the violence of men who commit some of the most heinous crimes known to society?

We must recognize the chronic batterer for what he is. If not, all of us become partners in his crime. Instead of being the victim's protector, we become her batterer's accomplice.

Summary

- Types of treatment include individual and group therapy, support groups, joint counseling, spiritual counseling.
- Treating the Serial Batterer is not encouraged. The best candidate is usually the Remorseful Batterer.
- Therapy might be effective for the Sporadic Batterer but only if he is highly motivated to change. If he drops out of therapy, he is almost certain to batter again.
- Treating an alcohol or drug addiction without treating the battering is not likely to stop the violence. Batterers often abuse substances in order to batter.
- Treatment for the wrong type of batterer could give the victim false hope and put her in greater danger.

Chapter 9

Treatment or Prosecution: A Critical Decision

"The night I left Bob for good, he had thrown an empty beer bottle through the TV screen, knocked me down on top of the broken glass, and punched and kicked me." Linda is continuing her tale of brutality.

"When he went to the kitchen for another drink, I managed to slip some money out of his stash and into my purse. I talked my way out of the apartment by pretending to get him cigarettes. Instead I got in the car, drove straight to a pay phone, and called the police.

"The police helped me get into a shelter for battererd women, and I stayed there about two months. This shelter offered me counseling, helped me find an attorney, saw that pictures were taken of the bruises all over my face and body, and helped me file battery charges.

"The shelter also gave me clothes I could wear to work, as I had run with only the clothing on my back. A temp agency found me a job. It was the start of a new life."

The goal is to get the battering to stop. Toward this end, the criminal justice system is a valuable ally.

Before I take you through the steps of using the system to your advantage, I want you to be aware of:

- why the criminal justice system is biased in favor of treatment for the batterer rather than prosecution
- how much pressure you will be under from the criminal justice system to go along with treatment for your batterer instead of prosecution.

A changing police response

In recent years, articles and television shows might have given you the idea that the police and the courts have a zero tolerance toward men who beat women. This is not true in all communities, even though changes for the better have been occurring in some communities.

In spite of all the hype about "get tough policies," in reality most batterers are not prosecuted or convicted for their crimes. The reason is that attitudes have not changed all that much: "wife beating" is still viewed as private family business.

To understand this attitude, it helps to look back a few years.

Before the 1970s in this country, the crime of wife beating went virtually ignored. Police were trained to go to the scene of a disturbance and play peacemaker or *mediator.* In some cases social workers went along to help partners resolve their "disagreements."

Before the 1970s, police seldom arrested the batterer or held him responsible for his criminal behavior. They often told him to simply "take a walk and cool off."

Victims of his violence were usually expected to manage for themselves. When the police left the scene, the batterer was free to continue beating his wife.

This kind of police inaction was severely criticized in the early and mid-1970s as women began to speak out about their rights.

Lawsuits filed against police departments by victims brought about some dramatic changes.

For the first time in American history, it seemed that crimes committed against an intimate partner were given the same importance as those against anyone else.

As a result, by the 1980s police began arresting batterers.

However, some police departments followed these policies only because the law forced them to.

Since 1990, the practice of arresting men for abusing their wives and girlfriends has increased. But in many cases, the arresting officers are not as well trained as they could be, and they might have too much leeway in deciding how to deal with the abuser.

My experience shows that if a man is arrested for beating his neighbor with a club, he is promptly arrested on a felony.

But if he beats his wife or girlfriend with the same club, he is booked on a misdemeanor—which carries a far lighter penalty.

Beware of quick and easy solutions

Before 1970, courts also treated wife beating as if it were not a crime. Like the police who had their instructions to simply go to the scene to "mediate" quarreling partners, prosecutors and court officials also preferred the role of peacemaker. They often dismissed cases of wife beating, saying that such matters were more suited to the civil courts, not the criminal courts.

In those days, no one took the crime of beating a woman seriously.

Over the last two decades, our nation's courts have significantly changed their procedures. But many court procedures are still unfair to the victim of battering.

Recent *pro-arrest* and *mandatory arrest* policies are leading to a huge increase in the number of domestic violence cases coming before the courts.

DEFINITIONS

arraignment: The reading of charges against the batterer in open court, where he has a chance to plead guilty or not guilty.

diversion: The practice of referring batterers to treatment programs instead of prosecuting them for their crimes.

dual arrest: The process of arresting both the batterer and his victim when both accuse the other of being the aggressor.

mandatory arrest: The policy requiring the police to arrest the batterer.

no-drop policy: A policy instructing the district attorney (or city attorney) that the preferred response to an arrest is to prosecute the batterer, rather than to drop charges.

> Note: Under a no-drop or pro-prosecution policy, the victim does not have to make the decision to prosecute—the DA does.

pro-arrest policy: A policy instructing the police that their preferred response to a domestic violence call is to arrest the batterer.

pro-prosecution policy: The same as a no-drop policy.

restraining order: A written order issued by a judge that tells the batterer not to contact the woman he has been threatening.

stay-away order, peace bond: The same as a restraining order.

subpoena: A legal notice requiring someone to appear in court to testify.

summons: An order to appear in court.

For every case that's closed, it seems two new cases are received.

We don't know whether more women are actually being beaten by their husbands and boyfriends today than in the past. What we *do* know is that more cases are being reported.

This is the result of more people waking up to the fact that violence against women is criminal.

Unfortunately, the huge increase in reporting is creating a large backlog of court cases. This backlog has led to new problems. All batterers—from first offenders to those who have abused women all their lives—are often handled in the same way.

As you are realizing, batterers cannot all be dealt with in the same way, because there are different kinds of batterers.

Batterers range from the man with poor coping skills who shows deep remorse for his one-time loss of control to the Serial Batterer whose lack of conscience enables him to commit murder and mayhem again and again.

Despite these vast differences, the courts often use quick and easy solutions to deal with the extremely complex and time-consuming needs of seriously disturbed Serial Batterers.

Such men get referred to counselors for treatment and rehabilitation, even though they are the worst possible candidates for treatment.

Seldom do professionals examine an individual batterer to find out:

- how remorseful he is
- how treatable he might be
- how dangerous he could be.

Without a proper examination by someone trained to look for these clues—or to detect the wide range of personality disorders shown by Serial Batterers—vicious and murderous men keep slipping through the system.

The process of referring batterers to treatment instead of prosecuting them for their crimes is called *diversion.* **It's the most effective way to reduce crowded court calendars.**

With diversion, some courts send the batterer directly to treatment, while others give the batterer a choice between:

- voluntarily entering therapy and completing a treatment program
- going to trial and possibly going to jail if convicted.

Which choice do you think most batterers make?

Treating all batterers the same gives those who are least likely to be rehabilitated a golden opportunity to beat the system.

The results are scary:

- The most untreatable criminal batterers enter treatment, only to drop out after a couple of sessions and return to their former ways.
- They get away with this.

It's very unlikely that the drop-out will be brought back to court for failing to complete a treatment program. That's because the court officials responsible for tracking these abusers are overburdened by an immense number of similar cases.

The diversion and treatment policies of many courts present a significant problem to you as a victim. Your life and the lives of your children, parents, and friends are put at risk.

Put your needs first

If you are a victim of a Serial Batterer, never suggest to a court official that your batterer needs help.

Unless you are a victim of Category 1 violence (or, in a few instances, of Category 2 violence), do *not* take the side of your abuser or try to get him help.

Even if you've never put yourself first—even if you find it uncomfortable to do so now—your needs must come first.

During a court trial, Frank's wife expressed concern for his well-being, even though she also asked for the court's protection from the man who had seriously injured her.

The judge, influenced by the victim's empathy for her batterer, gave Frank two years' probation and ordered him into outpatient counseling. Thirty days later, he was arrested again, this time for murdering his wife. He had never attended counseling. Nor had the system that previously convicted him ever supervised his probation.

It is easier for a court to divert a case to treatment than to prepare the case for trial and prosecute. So judges and prosecutors look for other ways of handling cases of abuse.

If you suggest that your abuser needs help, these judges and prosecutors will be eager to take the easy way out. They will dispose of your case in spite of:

- the danger your abuser represents to you and others
- the sick brutality of his crimes against you and your children.

Don't provide the courts with a "quick fix," because it can only work against you.

In addition, defense attorneys—who represent the batterer—generally grab any advantage they can to get their clients off. Their most common tactic is to say:

- "My client needs help for his drinking problem."
- "My client has a problem and needs help; jail will only make him worse."

Don't give the batterer and his attorney an easy out. It, too, can work against you. If you are approached by your batterer's attorney to make a deal, say you aren't interested.

You must be very assertive, otherwise you might later find that you have been manipulated and deceived, and that your safety is greatly endangered.

If you continue to put your abuser's needs before your own—*as he taught you to do*—you are enabling him to keep manipulating you, the courts, the counselors who provide treatment, and everyone else.

Imagine suggesting treatment for a violent man who severely beats his neighbor. Yet it's almost standard practice for a violent man who severely beats his intimate partner to be sent to treatment.

Violence is violence. Unfortunately, the criminal justice system in most communities still operates under a double standard.

If the man who batters you is a Sporadic Batterer or a Serial Batterer, you need a strong support system. That support system can:

- help you resist diversion—the popular practice of sending a batterer for treatment
- help you insist upon the protection you deserve from the courts.

Beware of poor treatment

When changes in the law made the police start arresting batterers, some people discovered a gold mine in supplying treatment to men who beat women. While many of the suppliers of treatment have a genuine interest in ending the cycle of family violence, many others have emerged with only a profit motive in mind.

There is much money to be made in the treatment of batterers.

Some of these counselors are qualified, but others have no idea what they are doing. Virtually anyone can "hang out a shingle" and declare him or herself a counselor. Some states monitor those who provide counseling; many don't.

Because the counseling field covers so many types of treatment, it's almost impossible for government to develop the kind of standards that would keep untrained "quacks" out of the profession.

Often as I go to and from court, I see "treatment brokers" walking the hallway of the court building. They are lobbying prosecutors to refer batterers to their agencies for treatment. These brokers make substantial fees from such referrals.

But when I talk with them, I frequently discover:

- they cannot define the term "personality disorder"
- they have never even heard of the basic tools that professional therapists use to diagnose such disorders
- they don't understand the extreme complexity of behaviors involved in battering.

Yet these "sales people" lobby for the release of a man who could one day kill you. They lobby for the referral of men they know nothing about.

We would not allow someone to practice medicine without a medical degree or license. So I believe we should not allow just anyone to "treat" men who, in many cases, are very, very dangerous.

Even a professional with impressive credentials might have no training or experience in the area of domestic violence.

Therapists who specialize in substance abuse are likely to see drugs or alcohol as the "cause" of an assailant's violence.

- These therapists might want you to believe that if the drinking stops, the violence stops.
- Similarly, marriage counselors might blame your abuser's rage on marital discord.
- Ministers might blame it on spiritual neglect.

My point is, unless a professional is really knowledgeable about batterers, he or she will certainly make a mistake in the diagnosis and "treatment" of these dangerously brutal men.

Misguided attempts at treatment could cost you your life.

Here are a few "mistakes" your advisors might make:

1. Some therapists believe that a batterer "learned" his violent behavior and can therefore "unlearn" it. They might take an educational approach, using lectures and

slide shows in an attempt to modify the behavior of someone who is actually severely disturbed. Whereas such an approach may be appropriate for Remorseful Batterers and some Sporadic Batterers, it is dangerously inappropriate for Serial Batterers.

A Serial Batterer can no more learn to overcome his severe personality disorders than a serial rapist can learn not to rape or a serial killer learn not to kill.

2. In many programs, the abuser is seen by a therapist perhaps 10 to 20 times for, at most, 90 minutes at a time. Yet we know that the behaviors of a Serial Batterer have developed over his lifetime.

   If anyone tries to advise you that such behaviors can be changed within such a short time, I suggest you find an advisor who's in greater touch with reality.

3. There is little agreement on how a treatment program defines its success. Is it measured by a decrease in violent behavior?

   If so, could a program call itself successful if a man continues to beat his wife but does so less often or less severely?

   Because the providers of treatment want you to believe their methods are very successful, they gather and interpret their own statistics.

   You don't need anyone to tell you that's a conflict of interest.

   • Would a program claim success in treating a serial rapist who eventually raped fewer women?

   • Would a therapist be successful if a serial killer just reduced the number of dead bodies he left behind?

4. Treatment programs that claim high "success" rates get their optimistic results by:

   • following a batterer over shorter periods of time than programs reporting less success

   • using official arrest records or the batterer's own reports rather than reports from the victims.

It's amazing that any study would rely on what a batterer says about his own progress, yet some do.

5. Finally, there's the problem of poor reporting by the professional who provides the treatment. For example:

- Some treatment providers rely on the batterer to report his progress to court authorities.
- Others use "fill in the blank" forms, which make it easy for an abuser to suggest that he feels remorse.
- Some neglect to report a batterer's attendance in the program.
- Some use the identical form letter to report the progress of every abuser they treat, merely filling in the name of the batterer in a blank space. The rest of the letter is the same for all, stating that Mr. _____ regretted his actions and was making progress in changing his behavior.

If this sounds ridiculous, it's more common than you think.

Yet the court gets the wrong idea about an individual batterer's progress and incorrectly disposes of the case against him.

If you see standard form letters giving feedback to the court in the case of your batterer, insist on more individualized reporting.

Even standard forms can be modified to contain more detailed information.

Many treatment programs do an excellent job with the right kind of batterer, and they provide victims with quality care and assistance. Model programs exist in Duluth, Minnesota, and in San Diego, California.

Although I support the existence of programs that are qualified to provide quality professional services, I am completely opposed to unqualified individuals who have no idea what they are doing.

They must not be allowed to continue endangering the lives of others.

Summary

- More cases of battering are coming to the attention of the courts than ever before. As a result, the courts are eager to dispose of cases by diverting batterers to treatment rather than prosecuting them for their crimes.
- Diversion permits some of the most vicious and murderous men to slip through the system.
- A victim must put her needs first and refuse to make deals to help a batterer who may be a poor candidate for treatment.
- A strong support system can help the victim resist diversion.
- Claims of success in treating batterers are often unreliable. Not all states monitor those who provide counseling. Some courts rely on the batterer to report his own progress.

Chapter 10

How to Get the Police and Courts to Help

Each time Cathy threatened to leave him, Richard ma-
nipulated her into staying and brought her candy and
flowers. Each time, all his promises to see a counselor
were broken, and the vicious beatings started again.

One time when he threatened to shoot her, she grabbed
for the phone. Richard threw a chair at her and pulled
the phone from the wall.

"If you call the police, I'll get you when I'm released.
And if you try to leave me, I'll take you to court and get
custody of the kids. Remember, bitch, you have no
money and nowhere to go. Go ahead, call the police.
I'll tell them you hit me first. Who do you think they'll
believe? Remember, I have two friends on the force, and
they'll have me released before the ink is dry."

Cathy ran into the kitchen, called 911 from the cordless
phone, and waited outside the apartment for help to
arrive. It was the first time she had taken such steps and
knew there would be consequences.

When the police arrived, Richard was very cordial. "I
admit that my wife and I had a little argument," he said.
"She's been running around on me and was afraid to

face the truth. I work 12 hours a day and come home to a dirty house and no supper. You'd be angry too. Sure, I raised my voice. She tried to bite and scratch me, and I tried to defend myself. I never hit her, though."

"What about the bruises on her forehead and upper arm?" asked one officer.

"She fell over a table as she tried to scratch me. The bruises on her arms are from me trying to restrain her."

"Was a gun involved?"

"Absolutely not!" Though Richard admitted to owning a gun, he insisted he loved his wife and would never threaten her.

As Cathy observed her husband manipulating the police, she became hysterical. "If you leave without doing something, he'll kill me," she screamed.

"See what I mean?" Richard said to the officer. "I have to put up with this all the time. I thought about leaving her but I love her, and she really needs me."

Richard's calm behavior gave him credibility, while Cathy's emotional state suggested that she might be somewhat to blame for the "argument." As a result, the police cited both partners for domestic assault.

After a sleepless night at a relative's, Cathy arrived for her arraignment. She was alone. She had no support system or advocate. She could not afford a private attorney, and though she had tried to get last-minute legal advice from a public assistance program, the waiting list was a month long and she hadn't made any arrangements in advance.

When Richard walked into the courtroom he was meticulously dressed and relaxed, and he made a point of sitting immediately behind his wife. A distinguished-looking attorney approached him. "I'm here to help you take care of your little problem," he said. "Let's go into the back and speak to the city prosecutor."

Cathy sat frozen in her chair until her name was called to come to the office of the prosecutor. As she entered, Richard's attorney began to control the discussion, praising his client as a hard-working professional who always provided for his family—clearly not a wife-beater.

"If anyone is to blame, it's Richard's wife," the attorney said. "That's why the police charged her as well as my client, who was only defending himself. He agrees, however, that if she is willing to drop her charges against him, he is also willing to drop his case against her."

As Cathy stood in bewilderment, the prosecutor said, "Ma'am, by reading the police report I know what you have alleged. However, there is no corroborating evidence to substantiate your version of what took place." He repeated her husband's offer.

Richard's attorney interrupted: "If she does not agree to drop her charges, we would ask for this case to be set for trial as soon as possible." Arrogantly he added, "I will be forced to file motions."

In a barely audible voice, Cathy agreed to withdraw her complaint.

Richard smiled. "I thought you would see it my way."

Once again, Cathy had been outmaneuvered by her husband—and by his willingness to strategize and make use of the resources available to him.

Help is available

Whatever you decide to do about your relationship with your batterer, it's important that you set up a support system and make use of the resources available to you.

Among the most critical parts of that support system are the police, the courts, and your advocate—a friend, shelter worker, or other individual who guides you through the many procedures you will encounter in your efforts to live a life that's free of violence.

Call the police

If your batterer attacks you, immediately call the police and ask them to arrest him. If for some reason the police won't arrest him, insist on their issuing him a summons.

Although a summons doesn't put the batterer in physical custody at the time of the attack, it does order him to appear in court shortly after.

If you've been assaulted, never show any reluctance over having your batterer arrested or formally charged. Even the police officers who take the crime of domestic abuse seriously can lose interest if you don't follow through with your complaint.

It's very likely you will have to call them again in the future, so if you want their complete cooperation later, be sure to cooperate with them every time.

Never ask the police to just tell your attacker to go away or to take a walk and "cool off." This will *not* prevent his continued violence. It's very possible that just as soon as the police leave he'll beat you again.

Asking the police to play the role of social worker in cases of domestic abuse is inappropriate and dangerous. It also decriminalizes the abuse.

What your batterer does to you is a *crime*.

Many women believe that arrest will make a bad situation worse. They are afraid that the batterer will seek revenge as soon as he is released.

Actually, studies show that arrest and prosecution have a tendency to discourage most batterers, with the exception of the most relentless Serial Batterer.

The threat of jail is especially effective in reducing the battering when courts put limits on a batterer's behavior and then monitor those limits.

Instead of being afraid to insist on your batterer's arrest, rely on your support system and safety plan to give you the confidence to press criminal charges against him.

When the police arrive

1. If you or your children have been injured, ask for the help of paramedics or ask to be escorted to the hospital for medical attention.
   - Tell the paramedics or doctors exactly what happened.
   - Always request that a copy of the medical examination be included with the police report.
   - If the police have a camera, ask them to photograph any signs of abuse, such as bruises or cuts that you or your children have. Ask the police to include those pictures with their report.
2. Ask the police to also take pictures of your property damage to include with their report. If you have a Polaroid camera available, have someone take two sets of photos. Give one set to the police and keep the second set for your personal files.
3. If your children witnessed the attack on you, ask the police to speak to the children in private.
   Never let the police interview your children in front of a batterer, because he will intimidate them.
   The police should record each child's statement exactly as reported.
   Children are usually very truthful in such situations. They generally report events exactly as they happened.
   Though I'm strongly opposed to having a young child go through the trauma of testifying in court, having the child's statement in the police report will back up the rest of the report. This can help you in court.
4. When you are interviewed by the police, always ask to speak to them alone. If your batterer is allowed in the same room when you are being interviewed, his physical presence could intimidate you and affect what you say to the police.

What to tell the police

1. Tell the police in detail what your batterer did during his attack on you. Ask to be allowed to submit your own written statement in addition.
2. Tell the police the names, addresses, and phone numbers of all witnesses who were present at the time of the attack.
3. Ask all witnesses to give the police a detailed verbal statement about your batterer's attack. Ask that the main witnesses also be allowed to submit written statements.
4. Tell the police about any current restraining orders that were violated by his assault on you. Ask that all such violations be enforced.
5. Tell them of any history of being abused by this man. **Many officers will take the incident more seriously if they know a pattern of domestic violence exists.** Also tell them about any other times the police had to be called to your house because of an assault by this man. Although many police departments have records of past domestic disturbance calls readily available to them, some do not. A previous history of violence might make a difference in whether or not the police arrest your batterer for his current offense.

What to give the police

1. Show the police any and all evidence of your batterer's attack, such as broken glass, broken furniture, or torn and blood-stained clothing. Ask that this evidence be properly inspected and collected.
2. Ask the police to take as evidence any weapon used by your batterer in his attack and to make note of it in their report. Tell the police about any weapons your attacker might still have access to. Offer to hand over these weapons.

What else to cover with the police

1. Before the police leave the scene of the offense, always be sure you get an "item report number" that identifies your complaint.

   Without such a number, it may be very difficult to find your case when you try to get copies of the police report or other court-related documents.

2. If your batterer is arrested or given a summons, always ask the police to tell you the specific date, time, and place he has to appear before a judge. If the officers aren't able to give you such specific information, ask to be referred to someone who can.

3. If the police refuse to charge your batterer, the very next day go to your local district attorney's office, city court, or justice of the peace and ask to swear out an *affidavit* charging your batterer with the attack. Many of these agencies have a process for filing charges when no police arrest is made.

FILING AN AFFIDAVIT

An affidavit is a written statement that you swear to the accuracy of before a magistrate, a notary public, or another authorized official.

Often, you can file an affidavit with limited evidence, even though the amount of evidence you must provide to back up your claim could be different from one jurisdiction to another.

To file an affidavit:

- **Be prepared to provide your attacker's address so he can be served with a subpoena.**
- **Bring a witness with you, since many agencies will not allow an affidavit to be filed without the signature of another person.**

4. Whether or not your batterer is arrested, given a summons, or released, if you feel he continues to be a threat to you, ask the police to escort you to a safe shelter or to the home of a close friend or relative.

5. If you decide not to stay in the house where the offense took place, always give the police the address or phone number where you can be reached—and indicate that it's confidential. Many cases are dismissed by prosecutors because the victim moves after the attack and fails to give them her new address.

Avoiding dual arrest

Many communities have "pro-arrest" or "mandatory arrest" policies requiring the police to arrest someone when they respond to a domestic violence call. However, since these policies have been in place, there's been a dramatic increase in the number of cases of *dual arrest*—in which the *victim* is charged as well as her batterer.

Some police might arrest you simply because they are poorly trained; others might do so to show they resent the mandatory arrest policy.

If you are wrongfully arrested, contact your advocate and ask that he or she help you get in touch with the authorities able to correct this injustice. While you must be very *outspoken* in these efforts, avoid being *abrasive*.

Approach people in a calm and assertively professional manner, which makes you more believable. If you are defensive or hostile, you only add to their view that you may also be to blame for the violence that occurred.

Understanding the court system

There's a difference between criminal and civil court.
- Criminal courts deal with crimes against the person, such as battering.
- Civil courts handle issues of child custody, child visitation, and property rights.

If you are being abused, use both the criminal and civil court systems to protect yourself and your children.

Criminal courts

Misdemeanors versus felonies

After your batterer is formally charged by the police for abusing you, he has to appear before a criminal court on either a misdemeanor or a felony offense.

- A misdemeanor is a crime such as:
  - » simple battery
  - » simple assault
  - » disturbing the peace
  - » making threats
  - » trespassing
- A felony is generally a crime:
  - » that is committed with a weapon
  - » that seriously injures the victim or involves a severe beating or assault.

Felonies not only are more serious than misdemeanors but also carry greater penalties. However, even if your batterer uses a weapon and injures you in his attack, it's possible he will be charged with only a misdemeanor. **It's up to you to do something about this.**

Meet with the prosecutors and be assertive in requesting that they consider upgrading the charge to a felony. To support your request for upgrading the charge, be prepared to give them evidence of the seriousness of the assault.

Monitor the initial screening of your case

It's absolutely necessary to become involved in the case against your batterer right after he's been charged.

Court systems often deal in different ways with the early stages of such offenses, and their different methods can be confusing. Become familiar with how your individual system works.

If you don't, you could miss an opportunity to affect how your case is handled.

Sometimes cases are screened or reviewed before they are accepted by a district attorney. If that is the procedure, find out who is reviewing your case, and make an appointment to speak with him or her in person.

Shortly after his arrest, your attacker makes his first appearance in court for an initial hearing, called an *arraignment.*

Always be present at this initial hearing.

It's not unusual for district attorneys' offices and criminal courts to process several thousand cases of domestic abuse each year.

To keep your case from being overshadowed by all the other cases, be sure to get involved in your case early and stay involved.

By staying involved, you also:

- get the opportunity to discuss your circumstances with court social workers, prosecutors, judges, and other court workers who can help you
- are able to have peace bonds, restraining orders, and protective orders issued if they are necessary. It's unlikely you'll be allowed such input or receive a restraining or protective order at an initial hearing *unless you are there.*

I realize that staying involved in the case and keeping in contact with so many officials takes a great deal of time and energy, which you probably don't have. Also, the weekday hours it takes could increase your costs for child care and even jeopardize your job. At times, just phoning members of your support system can seem like too much effort.

Some days, the things you are responsible for can seem overwhelming, and you wonder if it's all worth it.

But if you don't become involved in the early stages of your case, it could be a long time before you get another chance to discuss your situation with members of the criminal justice system.

It's possible you'll *never* get the opportunity, because much of the review of the case takes place without your direct input. That's because under recent no-drop policies, the prosecution of your batterer is the state's case, not yours. You are considered merely a witness.

Never take your case for granted. Learn to assert yourself.

Otherwise, your case could be dismissed before you realize what's happening.

Be certain the prosecutor's office has your latest address and phone number. If you can't be found, your case will probably be dismissed.

Enlist an advocate's help

Going to court can be very intimidating, so ask your advocate to attend the hearings with you. She or he can give you emotional support and help you to understand a system that is both complicated and threatening.

If a victim assistance program is connected with the court, meet with its staff and ask that they help you as well.

As a victim, you do not need an attorney to represent you in such criminal proceedings. Your interest and safety are represented by city and state prosecutors.

However, if you feel more comfortable having your own attorney involved—and if you can afford the expense—it's helpful to have a legal advisor as your advocate. This is especially true if your attorney-advocate knows the prosecutor who's dealing with your case.

Tell your batterer's history

If your batterer has been arrested or convicted in other domestic violence cases, always inform the people who are screening and reviewing your case.

Never assume that a prosecutor has your batterer's complete criminal record, especially if previous assaults took place in a different city or state.

HOW TO GET PROSECUTORS TO BELIEVE YOU

Even when the police submit a complete and detailed report of the battering, you might still have to convince the prosecutors to believe you when you attend conferences or pre-trial hearings.

You will need to be assertive to get the court to agree to prosecute.

It's helpful if you bring the following with you:

- current and past protective orders, peace bonds, etc.
- court documents and case numbers of current and past criminal cases involving your batterer's abuse of you
- current and past medical reports describing injuries you received from your batterer
- current and past photos of the injuries, bruises, etc., you received from your batterer
- all bloodstained or torn clothing from the beating
- threatening letters or notes from your batterer, as well as affectionate notes, because they can show how changeable his emotions are
- audio tapes you recorded of harassing or threatening phone calls from your batterer
- photographs that show personal property he damaged
- any witnesses to the current offense or past violence
- any other items, documents, or people you can think of who will help convince a prosecutor that you are in danger.

Don't be afraid to prosecute

When you talk with prosecutors, always act determined to press charges against your batterer. If you seem hesitant, you might find your case dismissed, because court personnel often look for a chance to dismiss what they see as only a "domestic matter."

They have seen how women who have been beaten often deny earlier statements they made to police or play down the seriousness of what really happened.

If you change your mind about pressing charges, you probably believe you have a good reason. You may be expecting to remain in the battering relationship. Or you fear your batterer will look for revenge.

But experience suggests that if you drop the charges, you are actually in greater danger.

- Your batterer thinks you are weak and open to attack.
- He realizes there are no consequences for his violent behavior.
- You no longer have people in authority representing your interests and safety.

Pressing charges does not automatically mean that your abuser goes to jail. You can get restraining orders and other court orders to keep your batterer away. If these orders are properly monitored, they can often be strong deterrents to future assaults.

You've worked hard to get away from your batterer. Don't throw all that away by weakening in court.

The issue of pro-prosecution

In some states, the courts prosecute your batterer even when you insist on withdrawing your charges. This is called *pro-prosecution.* Although you may be the victim, it's the state that actually brings the criminal charges. If the state wants to go forward with the charges, you might not necessarily be able to withdraw them.

Here are two benefits of pro-arrest and pro-prosecution policies:

- They remove the burden from you of deciding whether to have your assailant arrested and prosecuted.
- They send the message to your batterer that it is the state, not you, who's responsible for any decision that could lead to jail.

Honor your subpoena

If you are served with a court subpoena, it's absolutely necessary that you go to court. Ignoring this court order could lead to your being cited for contempt.

If, for whatever reason, you are reluctant to follow through with your case, call the prosecutor or appropriate court official and explain why.

Talking it over could help you deal with some of your fears and uncertainties.

Keep in mind that you will probably need the court's help in the future, so you don't want to cause the prosecutor and your advocates to lose interest because you appear uncooperative.

Subpoena your witnesses

If any witnesses in your case were not listed in the police report, give the court their names and addresses and ask that they be served with subpoenas.

Even if your witnesses do not receive subpoenas, ask them to accompany you to court anyway. They can testify on your behalf.

Protect your safety in court

When you attend court proceedings involving your batterer, you can do three things to improve your safety.

1. **Ask the prosecutor or a member of the court staff to let you wait in an area separate from where your batterer is waiting.**

Usually, court employees don't recognize how intimidated you could feel sitting or standing in a crowded hallway with your abuser only a few feet away. Yet they will accommodate your waiting elsewhere if you ask.

2. **Except during the trial itself, you should never have to tell your story in the presence of your batterer.**

   If there's no privacy offered to you while you answer questions, be sure to *assert yourself* and insist on speaking to prosecutors and court officials alone.

3. **After each court proceeding, ask your advocate or someone in authority to escort you safely to your car.**

   Batterers often take such opportunities to intimidate and terrorize their victims.

If you feel you are in great danger, ask the court to place your assailant in custody.

Although his being held in custody might not keep your batterer from being released before trial, it will:

- impress him with the consequences of his behavior
- serve as a deterrent to future assault.

Get a restraining order

Restraining orders that instruct your batterer to stop harassing you are called by a variety of names. They are known as *stay-away orders, anti-harassment orders, protective orders, peace bonds,* or *temporary restraining orders (TROs).*

Although some are specific in what they order, others are somewhat general. However, they all try for basically the same goal: reducing or stopping the batterer's harassment of his victim and his threats.

These court orders are not issued automatically. Unless you request one, you are unlikely to receive it.

If a restraining order is issued, ask the prosecutor or the judge to set a *periodic status review.* This is a hearing that takes place about every three months in which the court reviews whether or not your batterer is obeying the restraining order. In some localities, such reviews are scheduled automatically.

Such hearings show the batterer that the court is serious about enforcing the restraining order, and they make the batterer more likely to comply.

CONTACT WITH YOUR BATTERER

When a judge issues an order telling your batterer not to contact you, it goes without saying that you should not contact him either. At times, he will try to tempt you to contact him.

Here's why you should avoid such contact:
- Any form of voluntary contact you have with him could destroy the value of the restraining order.
- You can also be certain that both your batterer and his attorney will use such voluntary contact against you in future court proceedings.

If you need to communicate with your batterer about child support, visitation, or other essential family issues, do so only through court proceedings or your personal attorney.

When a restraining order is violated

If a status hearing has *not* been set and your batterer harasses you in spite of a restraining order:
- Go immediately to the court that issued the order and ask for the violation to be dealt with.
- Bring your advocate with you, as well as witnesses and any evidence to back up your claim that your batterer violated his restraining order.

However, if a status hearing *has* been set and your batterer harasses you in spite of a restraining order:

- Consider waiting until the day of your scheduled hearing to discuss the violation—provided the batterer's behavior was not serious.
- If the violation was serious, ask the court to take immediate action. In many jurisdictions, police are allowed to take action whenever there's evidence that a batterer has violated a restraining order. In some cities, a violation of a restraining order is considered a separate crime.

Ask to be notified of release

If criminal proceedings do lead to the conviction and imprisonment of your batterer, here are three steps for you to take to protect yourself:
1. Always ask that you be notified before he is released.
2. Ask that special conditions be set to forbid him to contact you.
3. Consider asking the judge to *order* the warden to properly notify you before your attacker is released.

It's very easy for your abuser to be released from jail.

- If he's placed in custody before trial, he could be released by posting a bail bond or being paroled.
- If he's found guilty after a trial and imprisoned, he could be released early because of good behavior, prison overcrowding, or any number of other reasons.

It's important to know when your batterer is to be released so you can start up your safety plan again.

Here's what you can do to improve your chances of being notified when your batterer is about to be released:
1. Send a certified letter to the warden of the jail or prison where your attacker is being held.
   A certified letter:
   - proves you made the request
   - gets your letter put into your batterer's file, which prison officials look at before his release.

2. In your letter, clearly tell of your fear of the batterer and ask that you be notified before his release.

3. Give your current address and phone number so you can be notified. Say whether this address is to be kept secret from your batterer, and ask that the information be kept in a non-public file not open to him.

4. If necessary, you and your advocate can visit the offices of judges, prosecutors, victim assistance workers, parole boards, or any official who can influence the early release process in favor of your personal safety.

Make the system work for you

You may be thinking there's quite a lot you have to do if the criminal justice system is going to work in your favor. There is, and that's all the more reason for you to:

- build a support system
- get an advocate who can help guide you through the many steps
- be assertive in asking for what you need.

Help is there, so you don't have to do it alone. But the first step must be yours.

Here's how the system worked to help one woman stay free of her batterer—after she took the first step of leaving him.

Remember Mary, whose violent ex-boyfriend followed her and was arrested for attacking her in a park? Even if she hadn't asked me for help, the case involving her abuser would have been referred to me, because one of my primary functions as a court officer is to screen cases of domestic violence for the city prosecutor.

As Mary and I entered the courtroom for his arraignment, a number of inmates were sitting and waiting. One of them looked right at Mary and gave an arrogant smile. I knew who he was without asking.

To avoid allowing him to intimidate her and her children, I quickly escorted them to the prosecutor's office. I was pleased to discover that the arresting officer was already waiting for us and that the city prosecutor was reviewing the police report with concern.

After handing me the court file and introducing me to the arresting officer, the prosecutor asked me to take everyone into the adjourning office and to come back with a recommendation.

The documents given to me revealed that Mary's ex-boyfriend had been arrested numerous times for acts of violence against other women. I believed the court could be persuaded that a high bond was in order. It would keep this violent man behind bars until the case was settled.

After a brief conference with the prosecutor, I re-entered the courtoom with him and took a seat near the front. As I made eye contact with the batterer, he looked away quickly and asked for a public defender. Following a lengthy discussion between the court-appointed public defender and his new client, the public defender approached the prosecutor and me with a request of leniency. We replied that his client had a lengthy criminal record for violence and that we would not agree to anything less than incarceration. In addition, unless his client was able to raise the high bail bond that we were prepared to recommend, he would undoubtedly remain in custody until the trial.

As the batterer was informed of our response by his attorney, he became argumentative and hostile. I find that such negotiations often bring out the worst in batterers. Within 20 minutes, however, we were again approached by the public defender, who asked what our recommendation would be if his client pled guilty.

Having discussed such a possibility earlier in the city

*attorney's office, the prosecutor immediately replied,
"Three months in jail on the first count of battery and
four months suspended on the threat charge. In addition, I request that he sign a restraining order, with the
stipulation that he will have no contact with the victim
upon his release. If he violates the order, he would be
required to serve an additional four months."*

*As the public defender sat with his client to discuss
the recommendation and to remind him that he had a
right to a trial, the batterer gave us an intimidating stare.
The dialogue between the two became loud and bois-
terous. Within 15 minutes, the public defender approached and said that the plea-bargain offer had been
accepted.*

*After being read his rights by the judge, and with his
court-appointed attorney by his side, the batterer entered his plea of guilty and was led in handcuffs to the
city jail.*

*Three months later when the man was released from
jail, I had two deputies escort him to the bus station for
his trip back to his home state of Texas. Offered a bus
ticket and a ride to the station, he had agreed to leave
New Orleans and not return.*

*The deputies later told me that as he boarded the bus,
he gave them an obscene gesture. They returned the
same. To my knowledge, he never returned to the New
Orleans area. He knew we would be waiting.*

Civil courts

Civil intervention

Like criminal courts, civil courts can issue protective orders to keep your abuser from having any form of contact
with you and—in some cases—with your children.

If you are married to your batterer or he is the father of your children, start divorce and child custody proceedings in a civil court as soon as possible.

Child custody, visitation, and support can be decided only after a series of written petitions or personal hearings. Although your batterer may threaten to get an attorney to take your children away from you, such a result is unlikely. However, don't be surprised if your batterer is granted visitation rights or even joint custody.

Unless you can show that he presents a direct threat to your children, most civil judges don't forbid a batterer from seeing his own children.

Whether or not your batterer gets child custody or visitation privileges, child support is usually ordered. If he defaults on child support payments, he can be charged with criminal neglect of family, and his privileges of visitation and custody can be taken away.

When you need an attorney

Some legal issues involving your batterer you can handle on your own, but many other legalities definitely require an attorney's help.

Basically, your options are:

1. Hire a private attorney.
2. Get legal aid from a public assistance program.

Both options have certain benefits and drawbacks.

The advantages of hiring a private attorney are:

- You can demand more attention and time from your own attorney than if you use a free legal public assistance program.
- You are likely to receive better quality service.

The disadvantage is cost. Private legal assistance can add up to thousands of dollars. But if you can afford it, the service you get by hiring your own attorney could be well worth the investment.

Private attorneys who do handle domestic abuse cases generally charge by the hour.

To use your attorney's time efficiently, keep your discussions to legal matters only.

Don't be tempted to discuss your feelings of anxiety, stress, or other personal problems with your attorney. For emotional support, learn to rely on your therapist or advocate.

If you can't afford to hire a private attorney, consider these resources:

- a local public assistance program, which either doesn't charge for its services or charges on a sliding scale basis—that is, you pay according to your income
- public law clinics operated by local law schools, which might offer free legal help if you fall below a certain income level
- your local state bar association, which probably requires its members to perform a number of hours of "pro bono" (free) work each year as a community service.

The major *disadvantage* of any public assistance program is work overload. So many people are using these programs that clients are likely to receive limited time and service.

This is not always the case, however. In fact, attorneys associated with programs for women who've been battered can offer very good service because they are so familiar with the issues.

They are familiar with the most recent domestic laws, the courts and judges who enforce those laws, and the procedures that can help your case.

Working with an attorney who specializes in cases involving separation, divorce, custody, and other family issues is helpful, because such cases can drag on for years. That's one reason not all attorneys, private as well as public assistance, accept such cases.

Agreements about the children

When it comes to visitation, child custody, and child support, always involve the legal system.

Never negotiate directly with your batterer over these issues or make a "friendly agreement" between the two of you without the formal approval of civil court.

That's because your batterer will use your informal agreement as just another way to control you. When you are "good" and do what he tells you, he "rewards you" by paying child support or by agreeing to return your children after visitation. However, when you are "bad" and act independently, he ignores all his promises of financial support and even threatens to kidnap your children and harm them.

Informal agreements have not been legally approved, so they are not enforceable through civil court.

Also, if your batterer takes the children, the police are powerless to charge him or return the children to you without a formal civil order—no matter how long they have been in your physical custody. So stay away from informal agreements. Your abuser won't honor them and will use them to keep control of you.

Child support

Formal court orders are essential when it comes to child support.

Nonpayment of court-ordered child support is a crime.
If your batterer won't pay:

- Ask the civil judge who issued the child support order to hold him in contempt of court.
- Go to your local district attorney's office and ask them to charge him with "criminal neglect of family."

The batterer's holding out on his financial responsibilities to his family is his form of control over you. Your court action to threaten his freedom is your control over him.

The federal government also gets involved. Civil court orders of support that are ignored can be enforced through the Internal Revenue Service. As long as certain procedures are followed, the IRS is empowered to seize your batterer's income tax refunds and to turn the proceeds over to you to cover the amount owed to you.

Child visitation privileges

If your batterer is granted visitation, ask the court to appoint a neutral third party to act as a "pick-up point" for your children, so you and their father can exchange the children without your having to face him directly.

Select a neutral party who doesn't live in the same place you are staying, so that you and others are not at risk.

Don't exchange the children with your batterer directly. That could give him an opportunity to violate the restraining order without getting in trouble.

"After all," he'll claim, "it wasn't my fault this whole thing happened. I just went to pick up my kids and she began to threaten me." Make it easy on yourself by always involving a third person in court-ordered visitation.

Victim compensation

Many states operate programs that enable victims of violent crime to recover some of the financial loss they incur as a result of that crime.

The rules and requirements are very different from one state to another.

To learn whether you might be eligible for some compensation, contact your local authorities, such as the department of corrections, the district attorney's office, or the sheriff's department.

If your state's victim compensation program does not include women who've been abused, ask your advocate to assist you in lobbying to be added to the list of candidates for such compensation.

Summary

- Whether or not you think you will leave your batterer, it's important to set up a support system in advance. Resources such as child care and public attorneys have waiting lists.
- When the batterer attacks, don't hesitate to call the police and press criminal charges.
- Studies show that arrest and the threat of jail discourage most batterers, with the exception of the most relentless Serial Batterer.
- Be sure that all evidence of abuse is fully documented, including photos, the medical examiner's report, and the police report. Tell the police if the batterer has any history of violence or possesses any weapon.
- Get an item report number from the police so you can identify your complaint and monitor its progress. Don't miss any opportunity to affect how your case is handled.
- Use your support system to keep from feeling overwhelmed by all you must do to stay involved in your case. Don't weaken.
- Understand what steps you need to take to ensure your safety, including how to request a restraining order and how to be notified of the batterer's early release from jail.

Chapter 11

Should This Relationship Be Saved?

"My husband promised to take the children to the movies on Friday night," Bea explains. "He'd been paid that afternoon, and the kids were dressed and waiting for him to pick them up. He didn't show, and about 10 o'clock, they got undressed and went to bed. They didn't even cry. They were used to broken promises.

"Late Saturday afternoon he finally showed up. It was obvious he'd been drinking again. He explained that he had been in a dice game and was trying to win his money back. He said he still planned on taking the kids to the movies but needed me to lend him some money until he got paid again. I reminded him that the money I had was borrowed from my mother to pay our rent. We'd been threatened with eviction, and my mom had helped us out until we could get on our feet.

"When I refused to give him the rent money, he became enraged, punched me in the face, and grabbed a heavy belt. He stormed into my youngest daughter's room and began to beat her with the belt while screaming that she was never satisfied. As I watched him beat my baby, I begged him to stop and shoved the money into his hands.

"As he grabbed his coat, he headed for the front door mumbling that he'd be back. I knew he would, as soon as the money was gone."

What does the future hold?

About the only hopeful thing we can say about the behavior of the batterer is that he is likely to burn himself out—eventually. Like all people with personality disorders, he seems to mellow in his later years. This usually occurs in his fifties, sometimes in his sixties.

He doesn't become a nice person. He simply becomes less mean.

Any mellowing tends to happen in the last chapter of his life. Usually, this is also the last chapter of his victim's natural life. If you are that victim, can you afford to wait? Should you? Will you survive long enough to have that choice?

Perhaps you are coming to realize that even if your batterer gets therapy, the beatings won't stop. In most cases, that's true.

Perhaps you are recognizing that even if the criminal justice system operates perfectly, your batterer won't be locked up for the rest of his life or yours.

What's left for you? Getting out—safely.

You might not like the thought of giving up on your relationship, and you might fear the difficulties you will face in becoming independent.

The alternative is to stay and experience continued battering, permanent injury, and early, painful death.

This alternative usually means permanent psychological harm to your children, as well.

Children of violence

A woman came to my office in the courthouse one day. Her partner had clubbed her in front of her baby.

As she sat cradling the baby in her bruised arms, she said, "When my daughter grows up I'm going to tell her all about this."
I responded, "You won't have to, she already knows."

The greatest mistake most victims of battering make about their children is to think they don't know what's going on.

Never underestimate the effect of family violence on your children.

If you are a mother who is habitually abused, stop justifying the batterer's behavior and start breaking through your denial of what that abuse is doing to your children—even if they are not threatened physically.

Research shows that family violence almost always causes permanent emotional damage to children.

Children notice far more of what goes on around them than adults do, and far more than we think they do. The fact is, they hear and see everything, whether or not they let their awareness show.

When my son and I take walks in our neighborhood, I am always impressed by Justin's seeing things around him that I no longer see. He reacts to the bugs in the grass and makes comments about the shape of gravel on the ground. He questions me about the flying birds and the setting sun. He notices the trees lining the street and the blooming flowers.

Children have an amazing ability to absorb even the littlest details of their world, even though our ability as adults to notice things seems to be blocked, perhaps by the stresses and distractions of everyday life. We have to realize that something as obvious as violence in the home affects our children deeply.

The psychological impact on a child of seeing one's own mother savagely beaten by the male figure in the household is beyond the ability of most adults to understand.

Growing up amidst violence

*I remember the four-year-old boy who told me that he
slept with a knife under his pillow "to protect Mommy
from Daddy." How could this child possibly grow up
normally?*

**No one can raise children in a sewer of violence and ex-
pect them to mature into emotionally stable adults.**

Bringing up children in a hate-filled environment often
makes them completely unable to have healthy, normal
relationships as adults. Research suggests that the earlier
and longer these children exist in such environments, the
greater is their emotional damage.

Even if you are considering putting up with the beatings yourself, consider the probability of your son growing up to be a batterer.

**The single greatest reason little boys become adult bat-
terers and little girls become women who are battered by
men is that they were brought up in a domestic war zone.**

If you need to motivate yourself to get out of an abusive
relationship, focus on the destructive effect that such violence is having on your kids.

Although getting out might represent an extremely dangerous decision for you, the decision to stay can be even
more dangerous and destructive—to you as well as to your
children—whether they were themselves battered or were
witnesses to your battering.

It's not by chance that the children of the victims I once
met in my court office nearly 20 years ago are returning to
my office as batterers and victims of their batterers. To see
this cycle repeating itself is the most tragic event of my professional career.

Violence is passed from generation to generation.

To repeat, if you are a victim of habitual abuse, take specific steps to cautiously remove yourself from such a rela-

tionship. Regardless of the advice from others to the contrary, a broken home is much better than a violent one. Children without a father are *far* better off than those who must hide underneath the sheets at bedtime because they fear their father will harm them.

There's no shame in ending such a relationship.

Keep this in mind: some families need to end. It's up to you to end it.

Children's counseling

As you begin to withdraw from your relationship with the batterer, recognize that your children, like you, need an opportunity to express their feelings and discuss their fears and pain. It's essential that they, too, get therapy to deal with the terror and trauma they have been through.

Much of the pain you have felt, they experienced as well. Like you, they undoubtedly learned to hide it.

Use your support network to learn of a children's counseling program in your area that can deal with their many needs. If you don't, they will almost surely grow up to be the next generation of batterers and victims.

When possible, avoid involving your children in court proceedings. Many victims bring their children to court for their own emotional support or to testify about the abuse that occurred.

Don't do it!

The additional trauma that such exposure could cause your children is not worth the benefits.

Besides, you won't need their support, because you will have a good safety plan that includes:

- **how to get an advocate to give you emotional support in court**
- **how to build a record of abuse to support your charges.**

Deciding to stay or leave

The decision to stay in a relationship or leave it depends on many factors. One of the most important is the likelihood of the violence continuing in the future.

To help predict future violence, one of the best tools I can offer is the Batterer's Continuum. It's based on the behaviors of large numbers of batterers, whose patterns of violence help us to recognize three very different categories of batterers.

Prediction for the Remorseful Batterer

We know that a woman who chooses to stay with a man who fits the profile of the Remorseful Batterer is unlikely to be beaten again, especially if he receives counseling.

Prediction for the Serial Batterer

The outcome of staying in a relationship with a Serial Batterer is equally certain. It's as certain as falling into a pit with a poisonous snake. If you found yourself in a snake pit, you'd know you had two choices:

1. You could choose to stay in the snake pit, sit quietly, and try to avoid being attacked. Or:
2. You could protect yourself with whatever you could find, then try to get out.

If you choose the first option, you don't have to wonder about whether the snake will attack you, only when.

If you choose the second option, getting out, the more protection you've been able to gather for your getaway, the less likely you'll be harmed.

A relationship with a Serial Batterer presents the same two choices as a snake pit, and the same certainty of results.

Prediction for the Sporadic Batterer

We can describe the current behavior of the Sporadic Batterer—the man who falls between the extremes of categories 1 and 3. But we cannot predict the future behavior of the entire category of Sporadic Batterers as we can with either Category 1 or Category 3.

Category 2 is very broad. It encompasses the majority of batterers in the United States. These hundreds of thousands of unpredictable abusers exhibit a wide range of character defects and violent behaviors.

Staying in a relationship with such a man is extremely risky.

So I urge any woman who is hoping to stay in a relationship with a Sporadic Batterer to think long and hard about her risks and her options. Many of these men are capable of seriously injuring—even killing—their intimate partners and children. Ending the relationship is usually the right thing to do.

If your family, friends, or counselors encourage you to stay in such a relationship while your batterer gets "help," you need to question their lack of insight.

Never buy into the suggestion that if your batterer enters treatment he is likely to change.

Change is always possible, of course. But the experience of most women who remain with Sporadic Batterers indicates that *at some point the violent and destructive behavior occurs again.*

In the vast majority of cases, the Category 2 batterer will not change his behavior.

If you try to "fix" him he might kill you while you wait. If you allow yourself to be manipulated back into a relationship with him, you are very likely to be beaten again—even murdered.

Hoping a Category 2 or 3 batterer will change is the worst reason to stay in a relationship with him.

"I lived with a guy for a couple of months before he started to beat me," explains Joan. "Whenever he didn't get his way, he would get really mad and threaten me

*with a knife or gun or his fists. I got out of the relation-
ship as soon as I could. It wasn't easy, but I managed to
escape by leaving the state and not letting anyone know
where I was going.*

*"Several months after, I was reading the morning news-
paper while having coffee and was shocked to read that
he had decapitated a woman's body, stuffed her head in
a garbage bag, and placed it on his new girlfriend's
kitchen table! That headless woman could very well
have been me!"*

It's difficult to advise the victim of a Sporadic Batterer
whether to stay in her violent relationship or end it.

Many professionals advise women to stay in abusive
relationships, especially if the batterer has agreed to enter
treatment. However, I have worked with batterers and their
victims for 20 years, and I would never encourage an abused
woman to continue such a relationship.

Each night you go to bed wondering when your batterer
is going to injure you again.

**Life is too short. You deserve more. Equally important,
your children deserve more.**

Type of batterer	Should you stay?
1. Remorseful Batterer	If you want to.
2. Sporadic Batterer	Not encouraged.
3. Serial Batterer	Strongly discouraged.

If you are still undecided, or if you've decided to stay
with your batterer if he enters therapy, have a safety plan.

Who needs a safety plan?

Generally, the wife or girlfriend of a Remorseful Batterer who is in treatment probably doesn't need a plan.

At the other extreme, even if a Serial Batterer is going
through the motions of getting therapy, it's *essential* that

his victim set up a complete support system and safety plan and be fully prepared to run for her life.

With a Sporadic Batterer, the woman is wise to develop a safety plan and have it ready at all times, whether or not she plans to end the relationship.

The likelihood of her having to use that safety plan depends on whether her abuser enters, stays in, and *finishes* a complete treatment program.

If a Sporadic Batterer does not enter and complete treatment for his aggression, he will certainly continue to beat the woman who stays in a relationship with him.

Special situations

Leaving the Sporadic Batterer

If you are thinking of staying in a relationship with a Sporadic Batterer, the best advice I can offer you is to give him an *ultimatum*—a clear either/or choice, like this:

"Either you get psychiatric help, or I am ending this relationship."

It's critically important to follow through after giving him this choice.

If he does not enter professional counseling, it isn't a question of *whether* to leave him. You *must* leave him. That's because if you weaken and don't follow through with your ultimatum:

• he will recognize your weakness
• he will see all your future threats of leaving as meaningless.

One woman who described a night of terror ended her story this way:

"Although I'd left him several times before, I left him for good that night. He said he would change but didn't. He promised to get help but never did. I understand that he's remarried. I pray for his new wife."

This kind of batterer uses manipulation to make his victim weaken: He promises to stop his violence *instead* of getting treatment.

If you are the partner of a batterer who attempts to manipulate you with such promises, do not put up with it.

His refusal to enter therapy ends all hope of his changing. Your choices become clearer: either leave or continue to be the target of his violence.

Leaving the Antisocial Serial Batterer

You need to be aware of special difficulties in leaving the Serial Batterer who has an antisocial personality disorder. Although most batterers who come before a judge are intimidated by the fear of jail, very little intimidates this batterer.

As the most likely of all batterers to serve time, he is also the most likely to go after his partner when he's let out, regardless of the consequences.

One batterer served 12 separate jail sentences for abusing the same woman. On his last conviction, the judge observed that the man seemed to be serving a life sentence on the installment plan.

Usually, women who decide to free themselves from their batterers have to assert themselves. But with an antisocial batterer, being assertive can make an already dangerous situation much worse.

It's absolutely necessary to take strong safety precautions.
If you are the wife or girlfriend of an antisocial batterer:

1. Establish a strong support system as described in Chapter 12.
2. Get a written restraining order that requires the abuser to make regular appearances before the court. This generally works very well but only within a court system that closely supervises its orders and jails the batterer if he violates the restraining order.

3. Consider arming yourself with a handgun
   - but only after taking extreme legal steps to stop the violence
   - and only after taking a certified firearms training class to learn how to use and store a gun properly.

I realize how controversial my suggestion is that someone might want to arm herself with a gun. But we cannot ignore the extreme danger that antisocial batterers present to their victims, especially those who have received little or no protection from the justice system.

The life and safety of the woman and her children could depend on how she plans to defend herself.

If a stranger continued savagely attacking you after serving several jail sentences for the same offense, wouldn't you take measures to protect yourself?

Summary

- Sometimes the only alternative to being permanently injured is to leave the relationship.
- Children are emotionally damaged by growing up amidst violence.
- The single greatest reason little boys become adult batterers and little girls become women who are battered by men is that they were raised in a violent home.
- There is no shame in ending an abusive relationship.
- One of the most important factors in deciding to stay or leave an abusive relationship is the likelihood of the battering continuing.
- With a Serial Batterer, the violence is certain to continue. With a Sporadic Batterer, the consequences of staying are uncertain, and therefore extremely risky.
- Hoping a Serial or Sporadic Batterer will change is the worst reason to stay in a relationship with him.
- Whether you decide to stay in such a relationship or end it, a safety plan is essential.

Chapter 12

The Safety Plan

"While I was in the shelter," Linda recalls, *"Bob failed to pay the storage on our furniture. So when the storage company sold it for storage fees, I lost everything—all my family pictures, keepsakes, furniture, etc. I had to start over entirely from scratch, and I learned that 'things' mean very little. One's life is infinitely more valuable than things.*

"I'm glad I decided to reach out for help to my friends, family, church, the battered women's shelter, and the justice system. I was determined to take advantage of the resources at hand and fight the battle to be free 'on my turf'—I didn't have to run from the city where I had a support system already. I just needed to use it and then rely on my inner strength, which I hadn't lost even though two failed marriages had caused me to doubt myself. Even a batterer like Bob couldn't extinguish that spark."

Linda adds, *"The message I would send to all women, no matter from what walk of life they come, is that domestic violence is unacceptable. There is no shame in seeking help. Money, furniture (I call it 'sticks'), and things like jewelry or keepsakes are nothing compared to the value of one's life.*

"We are not worthless, as our batterers would have us believe. We are strong, resourceful women. We can survive, even thrive, without them."

Once you decide that leaving your batterer is the only way to stop living in violence, it's important to have a carefully thought-out safety plan in place, ready to use.

Realistically, though, your safety plan might consist of little more than grabbing your children and running from your home in the middle of the night.

Your safety first

If your life and safety are not in immediate danger, delay your escape until you've carefully arranged to deal with many of the problems that you will run into once you are on your own.

Take the time to plan in advance:
- how you will leave
- what you will do after you leave.

I realize that the journey might seem overwhelming at first. But taking care of as many of the details as possible before getting out of your relationship is really easier than having to flee in the middle of the night with no clothes, no money, and no allies.

A woman who has to leave home suddenly, with only the nightgown she is wearing, is more likely to return to her abuser—and to more of his abuse.

With a safety plan, you are thinking beyond your initial escape. You are preparing for your future. Some day when you are embroiled in an exhausting court battle, for example, you'll be grateful that you set up your support system in advance so you have it when you most need it.

"The first time I left him he pulled a gun from the dresser and threatened to kill me and the kids," recalls Carmella. "So I just grabbed them and ran. I took nothing with me

because I wasn't prepared. I believed I'd never leave him, no matter what.

"We had no food, clothes, or medicine, and no money to buy them. We didn't even have a bed to sleep in. My husband refused to give us a thing. He wouldn't even give me the baby's diaper bag and bottles.

"I have no doubt he was trying to make me return. We both knew he had the power to do so, because we were so dependent on him for our physical needs. After almost becoming homeless, I finally gave in. I got tired of seeing my children hungry and sleeping at a different place each night. It was a choice between living in fear and living on the street. At the time, I chose fear.

"The second time I left, I was more prepared. I had started attending groups for battered women at a local shelter, and they taught me how to set up a safety plan. They gave me a list of things I could do before leaving and another list explaining what to do after.

"The plan made sense. In fact, the suggestions were so logical I wondered why I hadn't thought of them myself.

"I hoarded as much cash as I could without looking suspicious, and I moved some essentials from the house one at a time. When I felt I had gotten everything as ready as I could, I picked up the emergency bag I'd hidden in the closet, gathered the children, and left while my husband was at work."

Carmella adds, "This time we had a place to go, I knew which agencies could help us, and I had friends I could count on.

"Though I knew it wouldn't be easy being on my own, and that he'd start looking for me, I felt really empowered by having a plan and acting on it."

I'd like to be able to tell you that once you leave, your safety is assured. However, unless you have an extremely effective safety plan, it's possible you could be in as much danger as you are before you leave, perhaps more. This is especially true if your abuser is a Serial Batterer.

Most abusers become angry when they no longer have control over their partners.

Some stalk their victims and continue to threaten them. In general, you can improve your safety by:

- being well prepared before you leave
- being very careful after you leave.

But I have to tell you there are no guarantees. One woman might have all kinds of support and still be attacked. Another might have very little support and not be bothered at all once she leaves. Much depends on the abuser.

Nevertheless, having a strong support system and safety plan gives you:

- many more options for becoming independent than you think you have
- a feeling of self-confidence as you take charge of your own life.

A safety plan includes the steps to take before you leave as well as after.

Before you leave

1. Explore all your options for leaving. If you wait until there's a crisis, you might not have enough time to figure out what's available for your protection.
2. Find an area to live where you will have a strong personal and community support system. When you are on your own "turf" you are less likely to be attacked by your batterer.
3. Personally visit the service agencies in that community and talk with the people who work there.

If the man who is abusing you is a Serial Batterer, take as many of the following measures as you possibly can. With a Sporadic Batterer, alter these plans to fit your situation.

As a victim of a Remorseful Batterer, however, you might not need them at all, except in unusual circumstances.

Support systems

The heart of your safety plan is your support system. It's made up of individuals and agencies such as:

- friends and family
- domestic violence programs
- battered women's shelters
- advocates
- police
- doctors and hospitals
- counselors
- child care facilities
- employers
- banks
- the courts

If any part of your support system is missing, it's like an acrobat having a hole in her safety net as she prepares to step out on a high wire. So you'll want to connect with as many individuals and programs as you possibly can if you should need them later. They can help to provide a buffer between you and your abuser.

Domestic violence programs and shelters

The most critical part of your support system is a domestic violence program. To find one, call the local police department or district attorney's office, or look in your Yellow Pages under *Crisis Intervention, Domestic Abuse,* or *Domestic Violence.*

Also see Appendix A on page 219 of this book.

Often there's no charge for such services. The programs are run by professionals who deal with abusive relationships all the time. They understand the danger you are in. These caring people are there to meet your needs and give you a hand as you stop the cycle of violence.

Before you leave your batterer:
- Make a list of the domestic violence programs in your area.
- Include names, phone numbers, addresses, and the services each offers.
- Call each program and ask for an appointment.
- Visit with each personally. These programs could be essential to your future safety.

Here's what these programs can do:
- Appoint an advocate to assist you when you deal with the police, make court appearances, and have legal concerns.
- Connect you with housing and medical care for you and your children.
- Offer counseling services, keep records of your abuse, and give you a chance to share information in private.
- Provide attorneys who give free legal assistance or services at reduced rates.
- Assist you with child care. Usually:
  » Shelter residents are eligible for on-site child care, if available.
  » Other arrangements need to be made for older children.
  » If you are not a resident of a shelter, other programs can help you with child care.

Don't wait until you've left your batterer to start making arrangements. Get your name on a waiting list ahead of time.

The good news is that these programs give you support, reduce your isolation, and help you reestablish your identity. They also provide proof of your situation if you should ever need it.

When you make plans to leave an abusive partner, do so in secret so your batterer doesn't find out what you're doing. Never leave addresses or phone numbers of domestic violence programs or shelters where your abuser can see them. This includes not telephoning your home from any location that you visit or plan to use for shelter, because its number will be revealed if your batterer has a caller identification feature attached to his telephone.

Never share information with others unless they can be trusted.

Advocates

An advocate is a person who speaks up for you. If you are feeling trapped and alone, knowing that someone has agreed to help you can make you feel empowered.

Advocates are another very important part of your support system. They focus on your needs and give you emotional support. They encourage you and help you find ways to leave your abuser.

With the support of an advocate, you will build the strength to stay away from the abusive situation.

It's up to you to pick a person you can trust to be your advocate. It might be someone close to you, such as a family member, a friend, a co-worker, or your employer. Or you might be comfortable with a professional counselor, shelter worker, attorney, or victim assistance worker.

An advocate needs to be able to relate well to others. If an advocate is easily angered or is argumentative, he or she could turn others who want to help you against you. Stay away from anyone who will make more problems for you.

Advocates can assist you in handling police matters, making court appearances, finding medical care and shelter, and dealing with any other issues that might arise. With an advocate by your side, you are likely to be treated with a little more respect by agencies and other professionals.

Sometimes an advocate's presence in a courtroom is enough to make an impact, even without a word being uttered.

Often, a batterer is uncomfortable around advocates because the advocate knows what he's done. He realizes that advocates have an influence with authorities, especially if your advocate is an attorney, police officer, or someone who works with the courts.

The advocate you choose could be your most valuable protection from your assailant.

The police

Tell your local police of your situation before you leave. They might already know about the abuse. But if you think your batterer will make trouble when you move out, share your plan with the police in advance. Their knowledge of the facts will help you later in any legal procedure.

Talking with the police when you are calm, logical, and nondefensive gives you great credibility.

If you wait until you are in a crisis to talk with the police, they might see you as hysterical and irrational, and you could lose credibility in their eyes.

Ask your advocate to go with you to visit the police. If your batterer hasn't broken any law lately, the police might say they can't take any action against him.

Nevertheless, let the police know:
* that he's abused you in the past
* whether he owns any firearms
* if he's ever illegally used firearms.

When the police know this information, they might come to your assistance more quickly if you need them later.

Doctors and hospitals

If you are injured by your abuser, get immediate medical care—for two reasons:
1. You might have internal injuries.
2. Your medical documents can be used as evidence in court.

Ask the police at the scene to take you to a medical facility to be examined. Being escorted by the police instead of by the batterer, you will find it easier to tell medical personnel exactly what happened.

Even if your injuries are minor, go to a doctor so you have proof of the physical abuse.

Refuse to answer questions in a waiting room. Let whoever takes your history know you want some privacy. Ask if there's a nurse, social worker, or other staff member who's been trained to work with victims of domestic violence.

Also ask to speak to the doctor alone. If your abuser refuses to leave your side, you might not be able to answer questions honestly.

If that happens, as soon as you get some time alone, return to the doctor and explain your fear that if you had spoken the truth in front of your assailant, he would have beaten you later. Set the record straight by correcting any misinformation.

When you talk to medical people:

- Tell the truth about what happened.

  If you pretend your injuries were caused in some other way, your medical documents will have no record of your abuse.

  Even if you feel embarrassed or shamed, be as open and honest as you can with doctors and nurses.

- Let them know if you are pregnant so they can look out for the baby's well-being.

- Be cautious of a doctor's offer to give you antidepressants or tranquilizers.

  These just make it easier for you to accept what's really an unacceptable situation. They can cover up your pain but won't stop the abuse.

  Moreover, drugs of any kind can lead to dependency, which will only make it more difficult for you to act in your own behalf. If any doctor insists on your taking antidepressants or tranquilizers, ask to be referred to a therapist who specializes in spousal abuse.

- Ask for copies of all documents and records that prove your abuse, including x-rays, anatomy diagrams, and photographs. As soon as such documents are available, put them in a safety deposit box or at the home of a trusted friend.

Counseling

When you are feeling helpless and alone, having someone to talk to and share your fears with might be just what you need to make it through.

When looking for a counselor, you might want to contact a local domestic violence program. The program can help you find a counselor with special training and skills with domestic violence. Remember, in some states, almost anyone can be called a "counselor."

Before you talk with a counselor, make sure he or she is qualified.

Never enter therapy with blind trust. Always ask questions!

See a counselor when the batterer is at work or away. If you work outside the home, try to schedule sessions during your lunch hour. Tell the counselor not to call you at home or send mail to you at that address. Your batterer could find out and become more violent.

Child care

If you have children, don't wait until you are in a crisis before you begin looking for reliable day care. Some facilities have long waiting lists. Find out about all your options for child care before you leave your batterer so that your name can be put on a waiting list, if necessary.

Many nonprofit groups—such as schools, churches, domestic violence centers, women's shelters, and government facilities—operate child care facilities on a sliding scale basis, depending on your ability to pay. Some might be free.

Proceed with caution! Just because a facility is easy to get to doesn't mean it's the best place for your children. They have been through your nightmare with you, and they deserve to be protected by caretakers who will treat them with dignity.

> Provide the child care facility with any court documents stating exactly who is allowed to pick up your children. If anyone is added to or taken off that list, update your children's caretakers.
>
> Child care workers deal with many children, and you want to be sure that your batterer or a friend of his does not attempt to use your children to force you back into the relationship.

Employment

You might be reluctant to leave your batterer only because you are feeling controlled by him financially as well as physically and emotionally. To become independent and stay that way, you need your own money. So it's essential you have a job.

Working outside the home empowers you, leading you to economic freedom.

If you haven't been employed for a long time, you might find it difficult at first to find and hold on to a job, or to juggle child care and other responsibilities. And the job market can be very competitive.

If possible, take classes or attend a vocational school to get training, so you can offer an employer special skills that make you more valuable.

Vocational schools also operate job referral services. Publicly supported adult education centers usually provide employment counseling, whether or not you sign up for classes. Many of these schools and adult education centers also have women's development counselors who can put you in touch with other resources especially for women.

Use every resource available to you in your community, starting with your state unemployment office. Check the "government" section or "Blue Pages" in your phone book.

Although it can be a challenge to work your way through the voice mail at these agencies, here are the kinds of services you can find if you are persistent:

- job placement counseling
- bulletin boards of job openings
- classes in job hunting and résumé preparation
- referrals to additional sources of job-hunting services.

A job counselor can even call employers to find out your chances of getting specific jobs you've applied for.

Banks

Visit with your banker to deal with financial issues as soon as you've made the decision to leave your batterer. Explain your situation and emphasize the need for confidentiality.

If you have very little money, ask that the bank's customary fees and minimum account balances be waived or postponed until you are able to afford them. If your banker refuses, shop around for another bank.

Here are the steps to take in using a bank's services to become financially independent from your batterer:

1. Set up a secret savings account. If possible, secretly stockpile cash from grocery or household budgets to put in your savings account.
2. Establish a personal checking account in your name only.
3. Apply for credit cards in your own name.
4. Consider a safety deposit box for valuable items such as jewelry, important papers, photographs, and cash. The alternative is to keep valuables in the home of a trusted friend or family member.

5. Arrange for a personal loan in advance, if possible, because approval could take time.

Have the bank send your account statements and any other mailings to the address of a close friend, family member, or secret post office box. In renting a box, make certain that any notices of renewal are put in the box itself or sent to an alternative address.

Documentation

Keep a diary of the abuse you've experienced. Simply list dates, times, and places, along with a simple description of your batterer's actions. Write brief sentences that are to the point. If you can type the information, so much the better.

Keep this daily record where your abuser cannot find it, destroy it, and punish you.

Instead of putting all your documentation in one notebook, tear out one page at a time so you can take the written information with you and leave it with a friend, at work, or in a safety deposit box.

Also keep copies of the following papers in a safe place away from home:

1. *Medical records, doctors' written statements, and x-rays of your injuries.*
2. *Photographs.*

   Have these taken immediately after an attack as well as several days later, because bruising becomes more visible 48 to 72 hours after a beating.
3. *Letters and notes.*

   Even letters that don't threaten you can show your batterer's *pattern of instability* by demonstrating the range of his emotions, from affectionate to hysterical to violent.
4. *Police reports.*

   Get these as soon as available, because it could be hard for the authorities to locate these after time has passed.

5. *Court affidavits.*

   Ask for records of court proceedings as soon as possible.

6. *Shelter records.*

   Ask for copies of your own statements. These can be particularly useful because they are written by people trained to interview victims of domestic violence.

7. *Peace bonds, protective orders, temporary restraining orders (TROs).*

   Ask for a certified copy of all court orders that instruct the abuser to leave you alone.

8. *Phone taps and tapes.*

   Gather all telephone evidence that shows his threatening behavior, with dates, if possible, to show how long his abuse has been going on. Batterers are often very bold when leaving messages to intimidate their victims, so don't miss any opportunity to get him to prove your claims of abuse in his own voice.

9. *Hidden tape recorders.*

   If you can, get a tape recorder that's triggered by a loud noise, and put it where it is unlikely to be discovered by your abuser. It will record the verbal threats and other sounds of his physical attacks on you, thereby proving how much of a menace he is.

These types of documentation will help convince others of the danger you and your children are in and how seriously you need their assistance.

General tips

1. Plan where you will stay once you leave. If you can afford to, offer to share the costs of food, rent, and utilities with a friend or family member.

2. Remove the items you need from home one at a time, gradually and secretly. Your batterer might notice too many things disappearing suddenly, suspect your in-

tentions, and take his anger out on you. For a list of things to take, see Appendix B at the back of this book.

3. Pack an emergency overnight bag for yourself and your children in case you have to leave suddenly. Hide it where your batterer will not find it, or store the items you will need at a friend's.

4. Apply for food stamps, if you are eligible, and have any correspondence mailed to an alternative address. Consider storing emergency food at the home of a close friend or relative.

5. Make a copy of all essential keys and leave them in your safety deposit box or at the home of a family member or friend.

6. Train your children to call the police or run to a neighbor's house for help if your batterer begins to attack you. Play-act with them if they don't understand what they are to do.

7. Keep emergency phone numbers next to all phones in your home. If possible, program them for one-digit dialing. In a crisis situation, it will be quicker for you and your children to press just one number instead of dialing a complete phone number.

8. Just before you leave, gather all your batterer's weapons and take them to the police. If they don't want to take the weapons, tell them your life might be in danger. Many batterers will not try to get their weapons back from the police.

The more steps you take in advance, the better off you are likely to be.

If you are feeling distressed or depressed by all the things you need to do, keep these points in mind:

- You don't have to do everything at once.
- You can get help from people in your support network who care about you and want to help you.
- You do not deserve to be in an abusive and dangerous situation.

After you leave

Get counseling

Once you escape from an abusive relationship, it's essential to get counseling as part of a domestic violence program—or continue the counseling you have been getting.

Don't think of this as marriage counseling. Your main goal in getting counseling is to end a relationship that's very dangerous to you—both physically and emotionally.

The worst reason to get therapy is because you want to learn how to change another person.

The best reason is because you want to develop the identity, independence, personal insight, and strength it takes to defeat your batterer's attempts to manipulate you.

You need to be prepared for your batterer's relentless efforts to lure you back to him. He will give you money when you are broke and buy your children clothes and medicine when they are cold or sick.

He will go through "the honeymoon phase," bringing you flowers and promising that "it" will never happen again.

He is a master at manipulating you, so watch out.

> Tony appeared at his arraignment on Valentine's Day carrying a dozen roses that he gave to his wife, Gina. She became flustered and confused, just as he intended as part of his campaign to get her to drop her charges against him.
>
> Only the night before, Tony had kicked in a door and started shooting over the heads of his wife and child.
>
> The prosecutor asked Gina, "Do you want those flowers?"
>
> "Absolutely not," she said, admitting that she was afraid not to take them.
>
> The prosecutor reached for the flowers, discarded them, and said, "Sir, you have a $10,000 bond. Take a seat."

The counseling you get from a domestic violence program is essential in many ways:
- It helps you recognize your batterer's manipulative methods.
- It gives you a sense of belonging to a community that cares about you and understands everything you are up against.
- It helps keep you emotionally strong, giving you the emotional support you need to make tough decisions.

It's not a sign of inadequacy to realize that you can't do it alone. I urge you to attend counseling regularly.

If you stop going to counseling, chances are high that you'll either return to your batterer or develop the same type of relationship with another batterer just like the one you left.

Domestic violence programs offer two types of counseling services:
- individual counseling
- group counseling.

Group counseling gives you an opportunity to talk with other women who've been victimized by their battering husbands and boyfriends. It can be a big help to talk with women like you who have been through the same thing. What you get from a group is very powerful.

Individual counseling gives you the benefit of dealing with your more private needs.

A domestic violence program is not the place to suggest that your batterer needs help. If you do—and if you are involved in a program for women that allows itself to become sidetracked into helping habitual batterers—you are actually helping your abuser get what he wants.

Let him look for services on his own.

Unless he fits the description of the Remorseful Batterer, if he's asking you about treatment it's very likely he is only manipulating you.

Stay in touch with your advocate

If you already have an advocate who is associated with a domestic violence program, keep up the relationship. If you've left your batterer but not yet found an advocate, find one as soon as possible.

Advocates can be a great help to you.
- They know how "the system" works, including the various agencies directly or indirectly associated with the criminal justice system.
- They often know the people who work in the agencies and in the criminal justice system.

Advocates connected with domestic violence programs are some of the most powerful people available to help you remain free of your batterer.

Your advocate can also be there for you if you find your will power weakening.

Get legal advice

Your need for a lawyer could increase greatly once you leave your batterer, especially if you have children. Child support, child custody and visitation, and various divorce proceedings cannot be dealt with properly without an attorney.

Domestic violence services can give you the names of attorneys sensitive to your problems because these groups often have attorneys serving as their board members, volunteers, or part-time advisors.

Use shelter services

When you use a domestic violence shelter to hide from your batterer, certain precautions are essential:

1. Keep the location of the shelter secret. Secrecy is absolutely necessary for your safety and for the safety of the staff members and other residents.
   - Never give your batterer the address or phone number of the shelter where you are staying.

- Never call him using the shelter's phone. Unless the shelter uses the telephone blocking function for its outgoing calls, your batterer could use a caller identification feature to track down the shelter.
- Never meet your batterer on or near the property of the shelter.
- If your batterer is allowed child visitation by a court, never suggest that he visit the children near the shelter. Instead, get the help of a neutral third person to leave the children with before and after the visitation. This keeps your batterer from having access to you while you are obeying court-ordered visitation.

2. If you have a peace bond, restraining order, order of protection, or a similar document from a civil or criminal court, give the shelter copies. In that way, if your batterer does come near the shelter, these documents enable the staff to call the police, have the batterer removed, and get the protective orders enforced. **Without such documents, the police might have difficulty taking action.**

3. Use the "buddy system" with a staff member or another resident of the shelter. For your own safety, tell your "buddy" where you are going and when you expect to return, just as you'd do with family or friends. If you change your plans in any way, immediately tell your "buddy."

4. Use whatever child care is offered by the shelter. It gives you time to look for a job or enter a training program so you can maintain your independence.

Keep the police informed

You know how necessary the police are for your safety while you are still living with your batterer. They are even more necessary after you leave.

Ending a relationship is a dangerous time, and the danger increases dramatically with your leaving. Therefore, let the officers who patrol your neighborhood know about your situation. This is especially important if you've moved to an area where the police don't already know about your problems.

Get to know the police *before* your batterer tracks you down. If you wait until he attacks you, you might appear hysterical, making it harder for you to explain the situation to the police.

Inform police of restraining orders

If you have protective orders or restraining orders in your possession, make copies of them and give them to the officers who patrol your neighborhood. In this way, if the police see the batterer on your property, they'll be able to enforce the orders even if you are away from your house at the time.

It's a good idea to keep copies of all such documents where you can get at them easily if your batterer does appear. Think about putting copies in the following places:
- in your purse
- near the front door of your house
- at the homes of family and friends
- at your job
- almost any place where you can get at them quickly.

Family and friends

When you leave your home and hide at the house of a friend or relative, you risk placing them in danger. Family and friends who provide you with shelter in their homes deserve to be as far removed from the batterer as possible.
- Never use their home as a way to continue the relationship from a distance.
- Never ask friends or family to negotiate between you and your batterer.

- Never ask them to help you get treatment for him.

The batterer becomes very threatened by anyone he thinks is interfering in his relationship with you. The more that friends and family appear to be interfering, the greater their risks.

If possible, go to a house your abuser isn't familiar with and park your car where it won't be seen by him. Being careful reduces his ability to find you, to damage your car, or to threaten your allies.

Public assistance programs

You might have to get some form of public assistance for the financial and physical resources you will lose when you leave your abuser. Women often hesitate to leave their batterers because most are totally dependent on them for money, no matter what their economic and social status.

Too many women stay with their batterers when they realize their standard of living will drop dramatically once they're on their own.

Of course, "standard of living" usually refers to "what money can buy," whereas a woman's freedom from abuse is priceless.

To remain in a violent, dangerous relationship is to choose a very low standard of living.

It's better to be poor for a while than injured or dead.

Public assistance can be very different from one community to another. Assistance is almost always offered by federal, state, and local governments, but it's also provided by private agencies, nonprofit organizations, church groups, and others.

Your local domestic violence program should be able to refer you to a variety of resources which can assist you in obtaining financial assistance, food stamps, and subsidized housing.

Your workplace

Keeping your job

Your workplace can be extremely intimidating to your batterer because it offers you the social contacts and money you need to become independent from him.

Batterers know that a victim without social and financial resources is a victim without choices.

So by harassing you at work, your abuser is trying to end these benefits to you and get control over you again.

Don't let him harass you into quitting your job—no matter what.

> **If you're worried about losing your job because your batterer is harassing you, go to your supervisor and explain. Point out:**
>
> **"I am just as much a victim as I would be if attacked by a stranger, and I should not be held responsible for the crimes and actions of another person."**

To get the full cooperation of your employer:
- Show by what you do and say that you are making every effort to stay away from your batterer.
- Convince your supervisor that you are trying your best to get out of the relationship.
- Never give the appearance that you are conspiring with your batterer or negotiating with him at work.

Phone harassment at work

If your batterer annoys you by phone, here are several steps you can take:
- Have a supervisor tell him that he's not to call you at the office.
- Have someone screen your calls before putting them through or be there to witness your calls.

- Install a caller identification device to discover where the calls are coming from and to document the time and date of each call.
- Tape all incoming calls made to your telephone extension by your batterer. If he leaves messages on your company's voice mail, tape them as well.
- Keep a diary of his calls and other forms of harassment.
- Take advantage of your phone company's free services for dealing with obscene and harassing calls. This includes putting a trace on incoming calls to determine where your batterer is calling from, although this might be difficult if your business has multiple business lines.

If he continues to call, file criminal charges through the police department or local courts. Telephone harassment is against the law.

If your batterer shows up

Ask your employer and co-workers to be on the lookout for your batterer and his intimidating, threatening, assaulting, or stalking of you on or near the workplace.

Ask them:

- to treat this man's behavior as a criminal offense, not as a private or personal matter
- to avoid getting into a conversation or argument with the batterer
- to remain calm if he comes to the office asking for you, and to avoid providing the information
- to immediately notify office security of his presence and have appropriate action taken, or, if there's no office security staff, to immediately call the police and alert them to the batterer's presence.

Making the workplace safe

To make your workplace as safe as possible, your employer can take additional steps, if practical to do so:

- Let you go to lunch with co-workers, if that's not now happening, or let you carry the company's cellular phone during lunch.
- Reduce the number of unnecessary entrances into the business, as long as the fire codes for exits are observed.
- Install an electric door lock and buzzer that allow a business to restrict who enters the work area.
- If there's an alarm system, install a secret buzzer that alerts the alarm company to a possible emergency.
- Establish a "secret code word" that would alert employees to notify the police in case you need immediate help.
- Install a closed-circuit camera system.
- Document everything sent to the company by your batterer: letters, notes, phone tapes, and anything else that will prove his harassment.

If the batterer is charged with criminal trespass or assaulting you at your workplace, ask your supervisor to attend court proceedings with you.

This shows your employer you are serious about getting out of the relationship. Your employer's presence in court also makes your claims more believable to court officials. Employers can make great advocates.

If restraining orders are issued by the court against your batterer:

- Ask that both you and your employer be listed on the order.
- Ask that your batterer be ordered to have no contact or communication of any kind with you or anyone at your workplace.
- See that copies of all restraining orders are placed in various work areas where they are immediately available to key staff people. If the batterer appears and the police have to be called, copies of restraining orders are especially useful.

Other safety tips

Keep documenting your evidence

- Continue to write down all instances of your batterer harassing you, as suggested in the first part of your safety plan (page 195). To convince authorities that your batterer is continuing to pursue you, you must be able to prove it. Never stop documenting.
- Continue to keep all evidence and documentation in a place where your abuser can't get at it.

Stay watchful and cautious

- Continue your "buddy system" by always telling a friend or relative where you are going and when you expect to return.
- Always remain extremely watchful when leaving your house, job, parties, etc. Never take unnecessary risks. Learn to scan your environment to determine who is around you.
  - » When walking in public, always be aware of who is coming toward you.
  - » If someone is sitting or standing near your car, don't go near it until you are certain there's no danger.
  - » If someone comes toward you from behind, immediately go to a safe place.
  - » If possible, have others walk you to your car. If there's a security officer at your job, always ask for an escort to your car. Most security officers welcome such a request. It also makes them aware of your problem and keeps them more watchful.
- Never walk alone. Your batterer is looking for opportunities to catch you alone. Most batterers won't attack you around other people.
- Tell your neighbors you have left your batterer. Ask them to notify both you and the police immediately if

they see him around your house. Early warning is absolutely necessary to your safety.

- Get a barking dog. It will alert you if an intruder comes on your property. A dog is one of the most effective early warning systems you could have, and a good investment.
- Consider moving out of the house you once shared with your batterer. He's too familiar with ways of breaking in.

Use technology for security

Today, many devices on the market can help you protect yourself. Consider these aids:

1. An alarm system installed in your house warns you if your batterer tries to break in. There are two basic types of alarm systems.
   » A local alarm gives you an early warning in your house.
   » A monitored alarm gives you warning in your house and also alerts others that you're in trouble. The security company monitors the system and notifies the police if the alarm is triggered.
2. Deadbolts for all entrance doors. There are two types:
   » A single deadbolt. Don't use this type of lock if an intruder can break a wooden or glass panel in the door and open it by reaching in from the outside.
   » A double deadbolt. When you are inside, entry to the house requires a key inside as well as outside, so an intruder cannot open the door by breaking a panel. This type of deadbolt is recommended, but be sure you and your children identify alternative fire escape routes from the house.
3. Locking devices on all windows and patio doors. Many types are available at most hardware stores. Such devices should never restrict your exit in case of fire.

4. Motion-sensitive lights, which turn on automatically when someone comes near your house.

5. Peepholes on all entrance doors.

6. Closed-circuit cameras with a connecting monitor in and around strategic areas of your house. Also consider a VCR to record whatever the cameras see. Place such equipment where it cannot be damaged by an intruder.

7. Fire safety devices. These are a must because batterers often use fire as a lethal weapon. Never minimize the need for fire safety.
   » Smoke detectors should be appropriately placed in your house. Your local fire department provides free safety inspections and recommendations, including escape routes and, in some areas, smoke alarms.
   » Second floors should always have a fire ladder.
   » Plan a fire escape route and practice fire drills with your children.

Telephone devices

Each of the following gives you added protection:
- A cellular phone to carry whenever you leave your house, giving you immediate access to help if your batterer appears.
- A cordless phone so you can place an emergency call if your batterer gets inside your house and you have to move from room to room.
- A telephone answering machine so you can screen all incoming calls before picking up the phone and tape all phone threats as evidence.
- A caller identification device, which shows the name of each caller on a small display screen *before* you pick up the phone. The screen also displays the time and date of each incoming call and keeps a large number of call records in its memory, which you can display

and photograph as part of your documenting evidence. In addition to the purchase price, there's a small monthly charge for the service.

- A blocking code, which you learn about from your telephone company so you can prevent others you call from seeing your phone number on their caller identification screen. The code is free, and you can get one whether or not you have caller ID service.

- An unlisted telephone number that you give to only a few very trustworthy people. Never make calls from your house without using a blocking code.

"After I left Bob, I moved in with a girlfriend who lived in the next town," Linda explains. "I stopped a police car patrolling the neighborhood just to let the officers know I was living there and what help I might need if my husband showed up and made trouble.

"Every morning when I got dressed for my new job, I put my girlfriend's cell phone in my purse. She carried her beeper and gave me the number. She also had a list of where I would be going and what time I'd return.

"The first week was uneventful, but I never let my guard down. However, as I was driving home after work on Tuesday of the second week, I glanced in the rearview mirror and was horrified to see my husband's car following me. As I looked at Bob in the mirror, he smiled arrogantly and pointed his finger at me as if he were pulling the trigger of a gun. When I stopped for a red light, he bumped me from behind. But when he got out of his car to approach me, I ran the light and kept going, fumbling for the cell phone.

"Bob jumped back in his car and chased me. I knew he carried a gun, and I thought I was dead. But I dialed my friend's beeper number. In a minute she called me back, and I told her what was happening and where I was heading.

"The next five miles were terrifying, with my husband tailgating me all the way. But when I turned into the subdivision, there was a police car waiting. I looked in my rear view and saw another police car directly behind Bob's car. I can't tell you the relief I felt. If it weren't for all the steps my friend and I had set up in advance, I think my husband would have killed me."

If you possess a weapon

Owning a weapon for self-defense is a difficult issue. However, in cases of severe and life threatening abuse where all other resources for protection have been exhausted, you might have no reasonable means of looking out for your safety other than obtaining a gun.

I don't advocate violence, but I do advocate self-defense.

If you must keep a gun in your house or apartment, don't store it in a place where it can be traditionally found, such as in the night table or under the mattress. If your batterer breaks into your home and knows that you have a weapon, those are the first places he will look.

Never purchase or possess a gun without first going through firearms training. Contact your local police.

The improper use or storage of a weapon can be extremely dangerous. Always keep a weapon unloaded, keeping the ammunition stored separately.

Lock devices can be purchased that prevent your weapon from being fired unless the lock is removed. They virtually eliminate a child's discharging the firearm by accident, even though they might slow you down in getting the weapon ready.

"For years I had been afraid to fall asleep," says Eve. "My husband would come home very late, drunk, and begin to beat me as I slept. One night, he picked up a brick and bashed my face in. I still have the scars. I began to condition myself to stay up all night, sleeping

during the day when he was at work. It was the only way I could defend myself.

"I realize that taking it into my own hands and killing him was wrong, but it was the only way I could protect myself. I called the police. I went to court. But he always got out, came home, and beat me again. No one seemed to understand.

"When they locked me up, I felt so much at peace. He could no longer hurt me. Even though sleeping on a hard floor behind the shadows of steel bars is not like sleeping in a hotel, it is safe. Finally I feel safe enough to sleep."

Summary

- If your safety is not in immediate danger, take the time to carefully plan how you will leave and what you will do after you have left. The woman who has to leave suddenly, with no safety plan, is more likely to return.
- Batterers become angry when they no longer have control over their partners. They can stalk their victims.
- There are many resources to help you create a support system so you can leave safely and permanently. Don't wait until after you leave to contact shelters, child care facilities, attorneys, and other advocates.
- Informing the police of your situation in advance gives you greater credibility than if you are in crisis.
- Keep good records of the abuse you experience.
- After you leave, get counseling for yourself.
- Get the cooperation of your employer in case you are harassed at work.
- To continue to protect your safety, use a "buddy system" and get as many security devices as you can, such as alarms, deadbolts, and a cellular phone.

Conclusion

It's Never Too Late

"Leaving Bob was a frightening experience," Linda says in concluding her story.

"Often, I seemed to make no progress. It seemed there were pitfalls at every step, along with ghouls to grab my ankles and pull me back down forever into the blackness.

"But taking one step at a time and holding firmly to the guardrails (my support system), I could eventually see the light and reach freedom at the end of the tunnel.

"I believe that with the help of one's faith and good support, one can go through the valley of the shadow of death and emerge victorious on the other side. I'm living proof. It's now been five years since my divorce was final."

Although leaving a batterer may be a frightening experience, women who have started new lives for themselves, like Linda, know how worthwhile their efforts have been.

Leaving is never easy. But the longer a woman waits before taking action, the harder it becomes.

That's because the woman who is systematically battered and isolated from others, and who has had her sense of self-worth destroyed, can develop a behavior known as "learned helplessness."

Learned helplessness

In an essay entitled "Battered Women and Learned Helplessness," the nationally known psychologist Lenore Walker
compares the helplessness felt by a woman who has been
habitually abused to the helplessness felt by animals in certain controlled laboratory experiments.

It could seem to add insult to injury to compare the reac-
tions of an abused woman to those of an animal. It's especially insulting when it's her *batterer* whose behavior is so
animal-like and inhumane.

**Batterers are the ones treating their wives, girlfriends,
and children in ways that you and I wouldn't dream of inflicting on any living creature.**

Yet much of what we know about behavior does grow
out of psychological experiments that could be conducted
only with animals, not humans—for obvious reasons.

I also want to emphasize that it's not my purpose here
to either support or oppose experiments using animals. It
is my purpose to provide you with information that lets
each of us make informed decisions affecting our individual
lives.

One scientific exploration that Dr. Walker reviewed involved newborn laboratory rats who were *trained* to be helpless.

Immediately after birth, each newborn was held in a
researcher's hand until it stopped trying to escape. Once
the animal gave up, it was released. Over and over the researcher repeated this "training" until all the rats learned
to not even try to escape.

They had learned to be helpless.

The experimenters then put the animals in a container
of water. Ordinarily, rats can swim for as long as 60 hours
without drowning. But most of the rats that had been
trained to be helpless drowned within 30 minutes. Some
didn't even try to swim, and they drowned immediately.

There's a limit to how much meaning we want to apply to human behavior from such laboratory experiments. So I will let you draw your own conclusions as I share with you the next story.

It was told to me by the sister of a woman who had been severely beaten by her husband over a period of 10 years.

"He beat my sister with chains, sticks, and rocks. He even beat her on their honeymoon. While she should have realized how dangerous he was, she always reasoned that he would change.

"My husband and I brought her to the hospital one night because she was having severe headaches and felt so fatigued. She died the next morning. I guess my brother-in-law beat the life out of her over the years. She simply lost the will to live."

Lenore Walker also looked at experiments in which dogs were placed in cages and given electrical shocks.

The important thing about the shocks was how they were timed—it was random. That is, shocks occurred without any pattern. No matter how the dogs moved or what they did, they couldn't avoid the shocks.

It didn't take long before the animals learned to give up trying. They had learned to be helpless.

Next, the research scientists changed the experiment so that only one-half of each cage received a shock. The other half of each cage was "safe."

But the dogs trained to be helpless didn't move to the safe half.

Moreover, when the researchers tried to teach the dogs to cross to the other side of the cage to avoid being shocked, the dogs wouldn't respond.

Even when the cage door was left open, the dogs refused to leave the cage.

They just sat there putting up with the punishment.

The researchers had to drag the dogs to the exit over and over again to train them how to respond on their own again.

Whatever conclusions you draw about the phenomenon of learned helplessness, I think you will agree that these living creatures were not at fault for learning not to resist.

Similarly, the woman who remains in her cage of violence is not at fault for doing so. She has learned the lesson that the person in control wanted her to learn.

Her feeling helpless is precisely what the batterer intended.

However, as a thinking, feeling human being, a woman can learn to *reverse* the training forced on her by her abuser.

The sooner, the easier

One more piece of knowledge to take from these experiments is that the younger the dog, the longer it took for the dog to learn to get over its training in helplessness.

Thus, for the woman who is realizing that leaving her abusive relationship is necessary, *the sooner the better.*

It is not easy to end any relationship, and it can be even more difficult to end an abusive one.

But it is easier if action is taken sooner.

- It can take longer for a woman to break free of abuse if she was brought up in an unstable home where violence was common. Her "training" had a head start.
- It can also take longer to break free if she leaves her batterer and then returns to him. Each time she returns, feelings of helplessness and hopelessness get a stronger hold on her. She becomes weaker and weaker, until, like the laboratory animals who have been taught not to resist, she no longer even thinks about leaving.

This does not have to happen to you.

No woman needs to live with violence. Every woman has the right to live in safety. Many, many resources are available to help you find safe passage from an abusive relationship. Use the information in this book to create a safety plan and set up your support system.

Remember: It is never too late to take action to stop the battering.

One woman decided to leave her husband after 20 years of marriage.

From the moment he got up each morning until he went to bed at night, he yelled and threatened her. The longer they were married the more frightening he became. He pushed her around, put his hands around her neck, and described in great detail how easy it would be to kill her.

"I could split your head in the bathtub," he'd say, and she knew she had to get away from him in order to save her life.

She also knew she had to plan carefully. The only time he wasn't glued to her was after dinner when he sat in the living room glued to the TV set. So each night after dinner when she took out the garbage, she walked past him carrying a second plastic bag hidden behind the garbage bag. In it were some personal items, which she carried, a few at a time, to the basement of their apartment building. There, in a storage room, an old suitcase of hers was stored.

She had given her escape a lot of thought, and she went about it methodically. She learned that the local women's center had a temporary place for her to stay. The center also gave her the moral support she needed. But she had to make the decision herself and carry it through herself.

She was 88 years old when she left.

As you can see, it's never too late.

Appendix A

Resources

FREE 24-HOUR HOTLINES

1-800-799-SAFE (7233)

1-800-787-3224 (TDD for the hearing impaired)

Above are the toll-free numbers for the National Domestic Violence hotline.

The hotline is staffed 24 hours a day by trained counselors who provide crisis assistance and information about shelters, legal advocacy, health care centers, and counseling available to you throughout the country.

1-800-656-HOPE (4673), press 1

Above is the toll-free number for RAINN, the Rape, Abuse, Incest National Network hotline. When you press 1, you are automatically transferred to the rape crisis center nearest you anywhere in the country. If you cannot find a shelter, this hotline can be used as a last resort.

Appendix B

Your Emergency Bag

Here are some things to pack in case you have to leave in a hurry...

- ❏ medications
- ❏ change of clothes for yourself and your children
- ❏ toys for the children
- ❏ names, addresses, and phone numbers of people in your support system
- ❏ extra sets of keys to your home, office, car
- ❏ cash, credit cards
- ❏ journal or diary, letters from the batterer
- ❏ police reports, court affidavits
- ❏ photographs of injuries
- ❏ jewelry, photographs, items of sentimental value
- ❏ other: _____

Here are other items you may need, but which might not be easy to pack ahead of time. Try to keep them together in case you have to grab them in a hurry...

- ❏ birth certificates, Social Security cards, other ID
- ❏ school records
- ❏ medical records
- ❏ insurance papers and medical insurance cards
- ❏ money, bank books, ownership papers for car and house
- ❏ other: _____

Appendix C

> If this book is not your personal copy, please do not write in this section. You may make one copy of Appendix C for your personal use.

How Dangerous Is Your Relationship?

Your answers to the following questions can help you decide how much danger you are in.

The more "yes" answers you check, the farther your batterer falls to the right of the Batterer's Continuum, and the more dangerous he is.

1. How long have you been with this batterer? _____

2. About how many times has he put his hands on you in any way other than in a loving manner? _____

3. Has he ever done any of the following?

   Pushed you around .... ❑Yes ❑No

   Slapped you .... ❑Yes ❑No

   Kicked you .... ❑Yes ❑No

   Punched you .... ❑Yes ❑No

   Choked you .... ❑Yes ❑No

   Pulled your hair .... ❑Yes ❑No

   Bitten you .... ❑Yes ❑No

   Burned you .... ❑Yes ❑No

4. If you are married, did he do any of those things before you were married? .... ❑Yes ❑No

   If so, what did he do and how often? _____

continued

5. Does he abuse alcohol or drugs? .... ❏Yes ❏No

6. Is he often depressed? .... ❏Yes ❏No

7. Does he have intense mood swings? .... ❏Yes ❏No

8. Has he ever been diagnosed with a mental illness?
   .... ❏Yes ❏No

   If yes, what was the diagnosis? _____

9. Does he stalk you? .... ❏Yes ❏No

10. Does he follow you? .... ❏Yes ❏No

11. Does he try to isolate you from others? ..... ❏Yes ❏No

12. Does he try to dominate you? .... ❏Yes ❏No

13. Does he monitor your behavior? .... ❏Yes ❏No

14. Has he ever intruded on your job? .... ❏Yes ❏No

15. Has he ever harassed you by phone or mail?
    .... ❏Yes ❏No

16. Has he ever threatened you with a weapon?
    .... ❏Yes ❏No

17. Has he ever attacked you with a weapon? ❏Yes ❏No

18. Does he seem obsessed with weapons? ..... ❏Yes ❏No

19. Has he ever threatened to kill you? .... ❏Yes ❏No

20. Has he ever threatened to kill others? .... ❏Yes ❏No

21. Has he ever threatened to commit suicide?
    .... ❏Yes ❏No

22. Has he ever tried to commit suicide? .... ❏Yes ❏No

23. Has he ever tried to hurt you when you were pregnant?
    .... ❏Yes ❏No

24. Has he ever sexually assaulted you? .... ❏Yes ❏No

25. Has he ever kidnapped you or held you hostage?
    .... ❏Yes ❏No

26. Has he had any previous violent relationships?
    .... ❏Yes ❏No

27. Does he have a criminal record? .... ❑Yes ❑No

   If so, for what crime? _____

28. Have you ever had a restraining order against him?
   .... ❑Yes ❑No

   If yes, has he ever violated the restraining order?
   .... ❑Yes ❑No

29. Has he ever missed a court appearance? ... ❑Yes ❑No

30. Have you ever been hospitalized or received other medical attention because of his actions? .. ❑Yes ❑No

31. Have you ever called the police because of his actions?
   .... ❑Yes ❑No

   Has anyone else called the police? .... ❑Yes ❑No

32. Has he ever damaged, destroyed or burned your personal property or your car? .... ❑Yes ❑No

33. Has he ever cut electrical or telephone wires connected to your home? .... ❑Yes ❑No

34. Has he ever broken doors or windows to get into your home? .... ❑Yes ❑No

35. Has he ever threatened to set you or your home on fire?
   .... ❑Yes ❑No

36. Does he intimidate and frighten you to control you?
   .... ❑Yes ❑No

37. Does he have frequent angry outbursts? ... ❑Yes ❑No

38. Does he have a difficult time when you are absent?
   .... ❑Yes ❑No

39. Does he accuse you of being unfaithful? ... ❑Yes ❑No

40. Does he try to excuse his beatings? .... ❑Yes ❑No

   If yes, how does he do this?_____

41. Does he hit your children or physically hurt them in any way? .... ❑Yes ❑No

continued

42. Has he ever threatened to harm or kill your children?
.... ❑Yes ❑No

43. Has he ever kidnapped your children? ..... ❑Yes ❑No

44. After reading this book and completing this questionnaire, which category best describes your batterer?

   ❑ Remorseful Batterer

   ❑ Sporadic Batterer

   ❑ Serial Batterer

45. Do you believe you need a safety plan? .... ❑Yes ❑No

Index

A